A MIDSUMMER WEDDING

MAY MCGOLDRICK

with
JAN COFFEY

Book Duo Creative

Thank you for choosing *A Midsummer Wedding*. In the event that you enjoy this book, please consider sharing the good word(s) by leaving a review.

❦ I *❦*

Stirling Castle, Scotland
Summer 1484

"IT'S YOUR WEDDING," the young queen said. "So why do I
feel as if I'm sending you to the gallows?"

Elizabeth Hay stood at the open window of the White
Tower, looking across the busy courtyard toward the chapel.
A hum of voices drifted up to her as worry tightened its grip
on her throat. The brilliant morning sun was shining down
on the castle's Inner Close. Along the walls yellow flags
with the red lion rampant alternated with the queen's new
flag of blue and white. The shadow of a bird drew Elizabeth's eyes to the sky. A hawk soared high above the castle
walls. Elizabeth wished she could grow wings and fly above
it all, her senses so sharp that she could know who came,
who left, who made promises, and who broke them.

Instead, the painful tightness grew into a knot,
spreading into her chest until she could not take a full
breath.

"Elizabeth," the queen persisted. "I'm worried about you."

The young woman turned to face Queen Margaret of Denmark, now the wife of James of Scotland. Known not only for her elegance and beauty but for her kindness, Margaret's concern showed plainly on her troubled face. Crossing the room, the queen took her hand, seated Elizabeth beside her on a bench by the window, and waved away the attending lady's maids.

"You're crying."

"Am I?" Elizabeth managed to say, unaware of the tears slipping down her cheek.

"Perhaps we haven't pursued every option. If you honestly don't want to marry this Highlander, I will insist on a postponement."

"Nay, that's not it," she began, faltering. How could she explain to the queen how she felt? Everyone assumed she was simply nervous about such a momentous step, worried about losing the life she was accustomed to, uncertain about the future. But there was so much more that Queen Margaret didn't know, so much that had transpired these past few days.

The young queen produced a silk kerchief and patted away the dampness on Elizabeth's cheeks.

The chapel bells began to toll. And now there wasn't even a moment to explain.

The time had come for her to go. Elizabeth stood and motioned to the other women to help her with the veil.

"I can halt the ceremony," Queen Margaret offered once again, putting a hand on her arm. "I can speak to my advisors right now."

"Nay, Highness. You're very kind. I know you've done all you can to help me. But the hands have been dealt, and fortunes decided. Come what may, I must go."

. . .

The Highlander waited in the Inner Close by the door to the Chapel of St. Michael. A congregation of nobles already stood inside, talking in hushed tones. Above their heads, blades of golden light from the slits of windows cut brightly through swirling clouds of incense.

Clan chiefs and lairds across Scotland knew that this union had been two decades in the making. Many wondered if the marriage would ever be consummated. It was an old story. A lass of three, a lad of seven—pawns in a contract when a fleet of ships was transferred for extensive tracts of land. As the years passed, anyone familiar with the two had hoped the families would find other means of satisfying the old promises, for it had become obvious to all that they were completely ill-suited for each other.

And no one had hoped for it more than the two young people themselves.

Macpherson frowned and edged into the shade of the doorway. Everyone in Scotland knew how different they were. Elizabeth Hay had been educated and brought up in the courts of Italy and Denmark. Now a close companion of the queen, she was well-traveled, fluent in several languages, and a talented musician. In addition to being a friend of the queen, she served as the indispensable right hand of her father, the well-known architect Ambrose Hay.

And he, himself? To the seagoing men of Scotland and England, he was Macpherson of Benmore Castle, the Black Cat of the Highlands, commander of a dozen ships that raided rich coastal towns and wreaked havoc on British, Dutch, and French traders. His chosen profession had made him a wealthy man. In seaside villages from Antwerp to Dublin, mothers evoked his name when they wanted to strike terror into their unruly whelps on dark nights. He was a Highlander. Wild, free, and dangerous. And for a wife, his closest allies believed, he would take a woman made of the same hardy stock. Not some delicate Lowland flower. Certainly not Elizabeth Hay.

And yet here he was, sweating as the bells tolled.

Macpherson glanced impatiently at the White Tower. Doubts ate away at him. She wasn't coming. This marriage was not going to happen.

A doorway opened across the Inner Close, and Queen Margaret glided over the stones of the courtyard, attended by her entourage. But he had no eyes for her. His gaze was fixed on the veiled bride at her side.

The young laird muttered another curse under his breath and scowled at the woman drawing near. The hell he'd gone through to be here at this moment. Had she suffered, at all? The embroidered veil hid any view of her face.

He did not speak until the queen and the rest of the bride's escorts filed past them into the chapel.

"M'lady," he growled.

"Highlander," she replied, coming to stand before him.

"Blast me," he cursed, taking hold of the veil and tossing it back away from her face. "You lied."

Seven Days Earlier

ELIZABETH HAY SHIVERED INVOLUNTARILY AS she stared at the deer brought to bay in the colorful forest on the large tapestry adorning an entire wall of the queen's chamber.

"That is not you."

"Nay," Elizabeth agreed. "My tale is captured on an entirely different tapestry. I'm in the one depicting the harried old sow, chased down and speared by a drunken pack of dirty Highlanders for my future husband's amusement."

Elizabeth turned and faced Queen Margaret, sitting with Clare Seton, one of the ladies-in-waiting.

The queen smiled. "I don't believe I've seen that one."

She nodded. "I'm not surprised. They only bring it out on special occasions. Don't want to frighten any of the maidens unnecessarily."

Elizabeth strode to the window, breathing in the damp air. Below, rain-soaked cotters from the nearby farms were already carting in food for the upcoming wedding feast.

"You may be allowing your imagination to run a little wild, my friend," the queen observed. "This is a rather dark vision of the future."

"A future that I'm desperate to avoid."

"Elizabeth, we've been through this."

"I know."

"Macpherson is a Highlander, as you say, but the man is acting quite honorably."

"An honorable act that I have no wish to be any part of," Elizabeth said flatly, trying to keep her temper in check.

Five years ago, she'd been ready. But where was he then? At eighteen, she was fresh-faced and eager, dreaming of the man she'd been promised to all her life. Innocent, believing in the power of love, she'd expected him to arrive and they'd wed and he'd take her to his castle in the Highlands. Trusting in life and the man who was to be her future husband, she had no fears, no insecurities. The future was an oyster with a precious pearl, ready for her to pluck.

But Elizabeth had dreamed of a man who never came for her. Year after year, her hopes faded. Doubt took root. Rumors reached her about her intended's legendary exploits . . . and a lass or two in every port. Sailing the seas, raiding rich towns, living a life of adventure. He was the Black Cat of Benmore. Terror of the German Sea.

Somewhere along those years, she stopped waiting and locked her foolish dreams deep within her. Time passed and Elizabeth traveled with her father, helping him with his work and learning his art of building. As a widower and a well-known and respected architect, Ambrose Hay made his home wherever his current building project took him. Together, they'd lived and worked in the courts of Europe. For Elizabeth, knowledge became a passion. Free of the burden of a future that depended on a husband, she developed a new life. A life that was hers.

In the end, Elizabeth learned not to want him. She wouldn't have him. She couldn't imagine giving up her life to be a mere laird's wife in a pile of stones in the Highlands. Without this marriage, she'd continue to travel with her father across the world. This was the future she wanted now.

But suddenly the Highlander had decided it was time. He'd come to Stirling, expecting her to be that naïve eighteen-year-old. Ready for him. Grateful for him. Ha!

Earlier that morning, she'd had a long and exhausting discussion with her father on this same topic. A month ago, the two of them had a future in place. He was commissioned to start a palace in France next June and he was taking her with him. This week, Ambrose Hay wouldn't hear of calling off the wedding. A contract needed to be honored. The family's name was at stake. Time didn't negate their responsibility.

Frustrated, she'd left her father with his plans and models piled high around him, and turned to her friend for solace. During their year here in Stirling, residing in the castle while her father worked on the renovations, Elizabeth had become a companion and confidante to the queen.

"Stop your pacing and come sit with us."

Elizabeth wished she could take the queen's suggestion, but she was too agitated.

Clare Seton looked up from her sewing. "You can't deny that Macpherson has made an effort."

Elizabeth glared at her. Whose friend was she? They all seemed in awe of the late-comer. Traitors.

"What do you mean?" the queen asked.

"The Highlander's squire came to the castle asking for Elizabeth again this morning,"

"Again?" Margaret asked. "What did he want?"

"The messages, twice yesterday and once this morning,

7

were the same. The laird wishes to meet with her. But she won't even send back an answer."

"Why won't you meet with him?" the queen asked, turning to Elizabeth.

"Because I know what he wants."

Margaret raised one eyebrow inquiringly. "And that is?"

Elizabeth had already explained the difference the years had wrought in her, but her friend's romantic nature would not budge. A chance at love transcended time and disappointment.

Queen Margaret had been a pawn herself in an arranged marriage, and she now lived in permanent estrangement from her husband. The queen knew firsthand the cold reality of the marriage business. If anyone should be able to understand Elizabeth's dilemma, Margaret should. But she didn't because she lived on the possibility of romance.

Elizabeth needed a different approach.

"Macpherson and I have never met. He simply wants to see me and appraise me as he would any property he was about to acquire."

"You could do the same," the queen suggested. "Perhaps you'll find out he's more than just the wild and uncouth Highlander you imagine."

Too late. Elizabeth didn't want to find anything positive about the man or this union. The mere thought of being shipped off to Benmore Castle to live among people she didn't know made her shudder. The idea of marriage no longer held any romance. She wanted to keep the life she had now. She wanted to go to France with her father.

Clare stopped sewing and laid her work in her lap. Even before Clare opened her mouth, Elizabeth realized she might have to kill her.

"The word already circulating the castle is that he's quite handsome," Clare offered.

"And he's a pirate," the queen added with barely concealed enthusiasm. "That alone speaks of a life of adventure and excitement. A real man. And I understand he's wealthy."

"Then he'll have no trouble choosing a suitable wife," Elizabeth responded, looking from one to the other. "He can find a woman of beauty and charm. Someone with a gentle temperament. An eighteen-year-old who would be submissive to his every whim . . . when he's not out robbing defenseless merchant ships. Anyone, so long as I am not that woman."

She couldn't care less what he wanted. She didn't want to know what kind of wife he sought. She wished he'd just go away.

"Come now," Margaret said gently. "If you feel that way, meet with him and tell him just that. Tell him you release him of his responsibility."

She couldn't. She'd never openly defy her father. Never bring dishonor to the family name. The Highlander would have to back away from the marriage.

Elizabeth wrung her hands and started pacing the room, unable to understand the panic clutching at her when she thought of actually meeting with the man and making such a request. Would he agree? Could she convince him? What would happen if he refused?

He had to be an arrogant blackguard. She'd heard the rumors. Alexander Macpherson was, by all reports, handsome and even charming. He'd been in Stirling only two days, and already there'd been talk of the man's great height, the intense blue eyes, the smile that made a lass forget her own name. He was accustomed to having his way with women. He took what he wanted, and he wanted this marriage. Why else would he come here now? He would never agree.

"I can't," she cried out with a plaintive look at the queen. "If only for my father's honor, I can't be the one who breaks this contract. But I don't want to go through with this wedding."

She paced the chamber, feeling as trapped as the deer in the tapestry. Each time she passed a window, she stopped and looked out at the workers, the walls, and the mist-enshrouded mountains beyond. The rain had been falling for two days, from the moment Macpherson arrived. Queen Margaret and Clare had their heads together, and they were whispering steadily.

"Elizabeth," the queen said finally. "Let's be clear on this. You want the Highlander to back out of this contract."

"That's it, Your Highness."

"But you understand that it's crucial for both of you to emerge from this with your honor intact," the queen continued. "Whatever happens, you don't want to start any rumors that might tarnish your reputation or his."

The situation was impossible. She forced herself to take a full breath. Tarnishing her reputation was not an answer. Her father's honor mattered. She felt helpless about what to do. Clare and the queen quietly exchanged a few more words.

Clare was the one who spoke up. "Perhaps we can play to the Highlander's sense of honor."

A last shred of hope. Perhaps he had a sense of honor. Would he listen to her plea? She doubted it. She couldn't risk it.

"What if Macpherson believed your affections already lay with another man?" the queen suggested. "Nothing scandalous. But what if he thought you were in love?"

"But I'm not. How could I conjure such a person out of thin air? And how would I make him believe such a thing?"

"We'll change places," Clare said.

It was impossible. Clare Seton was the queen's lady-in-waiting and betrothed to Sir Robert Johnstone, a wealthy Lowlander. People knew her. Her family was well-connected at court.

"You're certain that Macpherson has never laid eyes on you?" the queen asked.

"Never," Elizabeth replied. She hadn't gone anywhere in public since the day he'd arrived in Stirling. Desperate, she looked on in anticipation as the two women exchanged a conspiratorial look.

"This afternoon, I'm to meet with Sir Robert," Clare told her, "at Cambuskenneth Abbey."

Elizabeth knew her friend was to be married at summer's end. It was a love match, to be sure, and hardly the same situation as she was facing. She waited, not liking where this conversation was going.

"I think the plan is brilliant, Clare," Queen Margaret said, picking up the thread. She turned back to Elizabeth. "You will go and meet the Highlander where he's staying, introducing yourself as Clare Seton. While you're there, you will weave tales of anguish. You'll tell him that 'Elizabeth' has stolen your betrothed."

"That won't do," Elizabeth cried, understanding the game they were trying to arrange.

"Time is pressing, and Clare's plan is what we have."

The queen paused and glared at her, making sure Elizabeth was paying attention.

"You will accompany the laird down to the abbey. Hearing your tale of woe, he'll deny that romance because she belongs to him. You will tell him his eyes will prove her words true. That Elizabeth is in anguish over the upcoming wedding. She is meeting with her paramour this very hour at the abbey across the river."

"No!"

"Hush." The queen tsked her to silence. "At the abbey, Clare—pretending to be you—will be waiting with Sir Robert. When the Highlander sees 'Elizabeth' with the man she loves, he will be overcome and release her—er, you— from the engagement."

"But none of that is true."

The queen rolled her eyes. "Help us here. Help us rescue you."

Elizabeth bit her lip. This had to be the most ridiculous plan she'd ever heard. It would never work.

"When they reach the abbey," Queen Margaret said to Clare, "I expect you to be putting on a tragic show of love and loss."

"I can do that," Clare said.

"But I can't," Elizabeth blurted out. "This is far too complicated."

"Why? What can go wrong?" the queen asked.

A thousand things, she thought. "Macpherson is a warrior. This is certain to bruise his honor, and we don't know how he'll respond. What if he decides to approach them? Engage Sir Robert in a fight? What do I do if—?"

"I'll make sure my guards will be there to keep anything from getting out of hand," Margaret told her. "That is not a worry. But for this plan to work, you must do your part. Before he even sees them, you must convince Macpherson to take pity on 'Elizabeth Hay' and back away from this marriage. You'll need to do the lion's share of the work at the tavern and along the way."

So she must pretend to be someone else. Lie about a non-existent liaison. Fool this man with a ruse he might see through in a moment.

This was a hopeless plan. Elizabeth was in real trouble.

3

Two DAYS he'd been stuck here, and Macpherson was getting damned tired of the place. The inn where he was staying, just down the hill from the castle, was a ramshackle affair, but it was the best one in the borough, boasting fairly clean rooms, an actual bed, a reasonably honest innkeeper, and the best ale for twenty miles. He needed to be in Stirling, but the Highlander had no interest in staying with anyone who kept houses here. So he'd let the entire inn.

As Alexander sat at a long table in the empty taproom finishing his letter, one of the shutters of a window looking out onto the street banged loudly. The wind coming in from the southwest was rising. If he were at sea, he'd be taking in sail and preparing for a squall.

He looked over the letter. He was no lawyer, and certainly no poet, but it would have to do. Corking the inkhorn, he gestured for his squire David to return the writing implements to the innkeeper, who'd just carried in a fresh cask of ale from the cellars. The day had been uncomfortably warm with hard rain occasionally blowing through. Alexander thought for the fiftieth time how he wished he were breathing the fresh salt air from the deck of his ship or the clean mountain air from the ramparts of Benmore Castle.

He couldn't wait to leave the Court. The very air here suffocated him. The sycophants, panderers, fops, the cowards pretending to be warriors, the games, the women dressing to lure their friends' husbands, the painted smiles, the fluttering eyes. This was the place where virtue went to die. Summoned numerous times by the king to Falkland Palace, he was well-schooled in the poisoned atmosphere of the court. Stirling Castle was no different. And his intended was comfortably embedded in this festering climate. No wonder she couldn't allow herself to give notice of his requests.

The wiry young squire returned and stood waiting a few paces off while the Highlander read over the letter one more time and then folded it.

"Take this to the White Tower," Alexander ordered. "I want it hand-delivered to Mistress Hay."

"You know, m'lord," David said cautiously, "I shan't have any more luck getting this message to the lady than I did before."

Alexander glared at the young man. "You need to impress on the queen's guard that this is important. The blasted wedding is only seven days off. The letter must get to her now. Tell him, or whoever you talk to, that the content of this is vitally important to . . . to my intended. Now get your skinny arse up that hill to the castle."

"Aye, m'lord," David said, rightly sensing danger in his master's tone.

Taking up the letter, he bolted for the open door, nearly running down a shape that moved into his path from the street.

"Beg pardon, m'lady."

Alexander looked up in surprise at the woman coming into the taproom. The hood of her light cloak had tipped back, revealing golden blond hair bound in a thick braid that disappeared down her back. Her dress of deep green was belted with a sash of black velvet that matched the color of the cloak. This was not the baker's daughter, come to deliver the bread for supper.

She did not look right or left but went directly to the innkeeper, who seemed as surprised as the Highlander.

"Don't know what I can do for you, mistress," the man said. "But the inn is closed for the next sennight."

"Closed?" she repeated, perplexed. "But I was told that the Macpherson laird is staying here."

"Aye." The innkeeper nodded toward Alexander. "There's the very man himself."

The blond head swung around, noticing him for the first time. "Oh!"

Above her high cheekbones, large alert eyes fixed on him. Wide, full lips pressed together as she studied him. The lass was young, pleasing to look at, but from the set of her shoulders and the hands clasped tightly together, he decided she was a woman on a mission. She started toward him.

Alexander stood. "What can I do for you, mistress?"

She didn't see a bench protruding from beneath a table until it was too late. Alexander dove toward her as the woman's arms flew out to arrest her fall, and he caught her just before she hit the stone floor. As he lifted her back onto her feet, he realized he was holding her in his arms a bit longer than he should. And he wasn't complaining.

Pressed against his chest, she was all curves beneath the cloak and layers of clothing. Alexander's head filled with the most tantalizing scent he'd ever smelled on a woman. A combination of roses and . . . something else. Citrus flowers. Sweet memories of sailing in the Mediterranean flooded back to him.

With her feet once again on the floor, she tried to step back, but there was nowhere to go. They were wedged between two tables. Her attempt at sliding past him resulted in his chin brushing across the top of her head. The softness of the golden hair startled him.

By the time Alexander was able to look into her face, the woman's earlier appearance of determination was gone. Her face was flushed, and she was making a great production of rubbing a bruised knee even as she straightened her dress and cloak.

"Perhaps we should start again," he said, not trying to hide his amusement. "As I said, I'm Alexander Macpherson. What can I do for you, mistress?"

Her gaze was slow to rise to his face, but when it did he was caught by the color of her eyes. They were blue, but not the azure shade of a clear Scottish sky. They were dark blue, like the sea off the coast of Morocco.

"My name is . . ." She paused and cleared her throat. "I am Clare Seton."

The name meant nothing to him, so he waited for her to say more.

"I serve as a companion to the queen. One of her ladies-in-waiting."

Finally. The lass must have been sent by Elizabeth Hay. His haughty intended was at least acknowledging that he'd arrived in Stirling.

"I've come on behalf of your future bride," she continued.

His curiosity was aroused by the appearance of this young woman. Why would Elizabeth refuse even to accept a message carried by his squire but now send this lass? Either something was amiss, or here was yet another reminder of how unversed he was in courtly ways. In either case, now might be a good time to keep his nose in the wind.

"And what of it?" Alexander leaned back against the trestle table and crossed his arms.

"If you'd be kind enough to take a walk with me, everything will become clear."

Remaining where he was, he looked at her steadily and saw her squirm under the scrutiny.

"Only down to the river. Well, actually . . . to Cambuskenneth Abbey," she stammered. "It's not too far. Not a mile down the hill."

"Why?"

She looked away before saying in a lowered voice, "To meet with Elizabeth."

Alexander let her words float in the air for a moment before replying.

"Why not meet me at the castle? Or come here herself?"

"It wasn't possible. She had some business to attend to." The young woman was twisting her hands before her. "She was certain you wouldn't mind joining her at the abbey."

He didn't mind, but he wasn't about to admit it. Indeed, he was impatient to get this business over and done with. He'd walk from here to Edinburgh if he needed to. His ship was waiting at anchor off Blackness in the firth, and he was ready to be on it.

Besides, he mused, it would be best to do the deed in person, rather than leave her to read it in that letter he'd sent off.

But he didn't like being ignored, and something in him —the devil probably—was enjoying seeing this Clare Seton squirm a wee bit. He only wished it were Elizabeth Hay herself. Still, he wondered what they'd told this one to expect from him.

MAY MCGOLDRICK

"Actually, I do mind," he said flatly, turning away from her.

"But . . . but is it really asking too much to meet with your intended before the wedding?" the young woman stammered.

"Exactly what I've been thinking for the last two days," he replied, pouring himself a bowl of ale. "Is it beneath her to see my squire? She repeatedly sent him away without even a word."

"I am sure she meant no disrespect."

"And I mean no disrespect now. But if she wants to see me, she can come to me." He picked up his ale, dismissing her.

"You're being unreasonable."

"Am I?" he said sharply. "You have my answer. Be on your way."

No sound of rustling skirts. No steps retreating toward the door. Only the creaking of the inn's sign outside, swinging in the gusts of wind. Perhaps she wasn't so frightened, after all. He drank down the bowl, pretending she wasn't there.

"Please reconsider it," she asked in a soft voice.

He glanced over his shoulder at her, surprised by the note of dejection in her tone. Her head was held high, but she was strangling two fingers with the leather tie from her cloak.

"Even if you don't care to meet with her, I need to go to the abbey, and I assumed you would accompany me. I didn't bring an escort." She unwound the tie from her fingers, seeing she'd drawn his attention to it. "I would truly appreciate it if you . . . if you'd come with me."

Alexander looked into her eyes for a long moment. She was lying. She'd come here for some other reason. He was the master of a dozen ships. He was the laird of Benmore

18

Castle. He'd learned early on the need for being able to see through a man . . . or woman. He could recognize when a person was lying. And that was exactly what she was doing. But why?

His gaze moved downward, taking in the pulse jumping wildly on the smooth column of her neck. He was becoming intrigued with this Clare Seton and whatever her game was.

"I can understand if you don't care to meet her. But I know Elizabeth quite well. Perhaps you'd be interested in asking some questions about the woman you intend to marry."

Alexander tossed the bowl on the table.

"Very well, mistress, since you need an escort. And frankly, I'm getting tired of sitting here waiting." He gestured toward the door. "Lead the way."

🎋 4 🎋

QUEEN MARGARET WOULD LOVE HIM. Clare Seton might reconsider her nuptials. Every lady-in-waiting in the White Tower might drool over him. But not I, Elizabeth thought.

Well, perhaps a little.

She was twenty-three years old and she'd been navigating the courts of the world since she was a girl, but this afternoon—for the first time in her life—she was finding that she was not immune to men. At least not to this Highlander.

But why now? Why did he need to be so handsome? Intensely blue eyes, the lines of his face and jaw so perfectly carved, his nearly black hair tied neatly in the back and falling past his shoulders. How different he was from the genteel courtiers who wore the latest German fashions and fluttered about the women, attempting to woo one or the other with sweets and poems no doubt written by some Italian. Nay, this Highlander would have no time for any of that. With shoulders as wide as any draught horse, he was so tall he needed to duck to go out the inn door. A bit rough in manner perhaps, but Alexander Macpherson was beyond handsome and he was all man. And Elizabeth didn't miss the way others took notice as they walked past.

"Don't be a fool," she murmured to herself.

The wind was buffeting her, and the rain that began again almost as soon as they left the inn was falling harder now. Before they left the borough, it was coming down in sheets, driven nearly sideways by the gusts. She couldn't remember a storm so powerful.

Her cloak and hair were whipping about her. Elizabeth peered ahead as they descended toward the cluster of cottages huddled along the banks of the River Forth. Once they reached the bridge leading to the abbey, they might see Clare and her fiancé at any time, if they were still out braving the weather. In any event, she needed to be alert. But the man striding beside her was definitely a distraction.

The Highlander suddenly reached out and pulled her against him as a donkey cart coming down the hill behind them came dangerously close to her.

She slipped, and her face pressed against his side. His tartan against her cheek did nothing to soften the hard, muscled body. The scent of wool and leather and man filled her senses. This was the second time he'd caught her. She righted herself and pulled away.

When she looked up at him, Macpherson was glaring at the farmer in the cart, who appeared to be laughing to himself as he continued on his way.

She needed to clear her head. She needed to keep her mind on why she was here and what she intended to do. Before they reached the abbey, she had to convince him that he was better off walking away from the upcoming nuptials.

"Elizabeth and I have been friends for a year now," she said over the wind, encouraging him to ask questions.

"The Setons are an old family," he said, ignoring her

comment. "You're a respectable lot, despite being Lowlanders."

This was not the direction she wanted the conversation to go.

"Now that I think of it," he continued. "I've met a few of you in recent years."

Disaster, Elizabeth thought in panic. She knew almost nothing of Clare's family.

"How about Elizabeth?" she asked. "I'm told you two have never met."

He was looking at the sky, which was becoming darker and turning an odd shade of green. The torrential rain had already formed muddy streams in the road. Aside from the frown on his face, the Highlander seemed unaffected by the elements.

"Allow me to tell you about Elizabeth," she repeated over the gusts.

"No need. Tell me about yourself."

Her foot disappeared into a water-filled gulley, almost to her knee, and he caught her again as she pitched forward. It was impossible not to notice the power and the ease with which he lifted her and set her on her feet. It was also impossible not to notice that he was slow to release her. For an insane moment, his handsome face came perilously close as he adjusted her hood and pulled her cloak around her.

"How long have you been in the service of the queen?"

"A year," she answered. "And I'm to be married end of the summer."

"Who's the lucky man?"

"I don't think you know him. He's a Lowlander."

Truth and lies suddenly became a jumbled knot in her head. She tried to remember what she planned to say to him and what she'd already admitted.

"I assumed that," he responded. "What's his name?"

"Sir Robert Johnstone."

"I know him."

Damnation. Hellfire.

Why didn't Clare say anything about this? How could it be that she didn't know? How could Elizabeth take the Highlander to the abbey and show him a man he knew and a woman who was pretending to be her? It wouldn't work. She was doomed.

She'd tried to tell Queen Margaret the plan would be a disaster. She wouldn't listen. Elizabeth swore she would kill Clare the next time she caught up to her.

When her foot slid on the rock, all she could think was that the damned thing was smooth, it was slick with mud and rain, and it had no right being in the middle of a good dirt cart path. She cried out. As she flailed wildly with both arms and feet in the air, time seemed to slow to a crawl until her face was only a splash away from hitting the ground. How he was able to scoop her up before she landed was a mystery. But before she knew it, her face was nestled into the crook of his muscled neck. Her lips were pressed against warm, taut skin. His scent filled her, and the urge to let her body sink into his nearly numbed her sense of reason.

"You don't get out much, do you?" he asked. "Some wind and a wee bit of water, and you're helpless as a bairn. I can't imagine how many servants it took to convey Elizabeth Hay down this hill."

A tingling warmth shot through her. Finally, he'd mentioned the name of the woman he was to marry.

As he put her down, Elizabeth drew back, pulling her cloak tight against the driving rain. With her eyes riveted on the increasingly treacherous cart path, she began to walk, and he fell in beside her.

Panic again seized her as they reached the bottom of the

hill. She needed to set up the ruse now if there was any hope of it working. And that hope was fading by the moment.

"Elizabeth comes this way often," she said as they started into the ragtag riverside village. "Sometimes daily, I believe. There is . . . well, I should just tell you. She meets someone."

"Is Sir Robert in Stirling?" he asked, ignoring her.

"He is. But I've just told you that your intended meets a—"

"Where is he staying? I'd like to pay him a visit."

Was he deaf? Could he think more than one thought at a time? Apparently not.

Despite the storm, a surprisingly large number of people crowded the road to the bridge. Carts and a stubbly flock of newly shorn sheep slowed their progress. The bridge was just coming into view. Elizabeth's blood ran cold. They were almost at their destination, and she'd done nothing to set up the ruse Queen Margaret and Clare devised.

But the plan was shite anyway. Nothing was working. She might as well turn around right now, climb back up that muddy hill to the castle, and put on her wedding dress. What madness had caused her to think any of this could possibly work?

And what a delightful way to start their long, long, long life together. They weren't even married yet, and she'd already lied to him. Told him she was someone else. Damnation.

She needed to face it. She needed to tell him the truth. If there were no options and she was going to marry him, she simply needed to accept her fate—pirate husband, a hovel in the Highlands, death as a hunted sow, and all.

"Mam . . . Mammy . . . Mam!"

Elizabeth's head came up as two wet and muddy urchins

ran up and attached themselves to her legs. She leaned down and looked into their dirty faces.

"What's the matter? Have you lost your mum?" she asked gently, looking around, hoping the real mother was nearby.

A young lass, perhaps a head taller than the two appendages still clinging to her, hurried over. Instead of dragging them away, however, the girl took her hand, nearly tugging her off her feet.

"Come home, Mama. Himself is waiting, and you know how he is."

"What? Who is waiting?" Elizabeth asked, finding herself being pulled toward an alleyway. She looked over her shoulder at the Highlander. "These children must be lost. Let me see if I can help them find their—"

The rest of the words were lost as a lean hand clamped onto her arm and turned her around. "Blast you, wife. Why are ye not at home? And what are ye doing nuzzling with the pirate?"

Elizabeth gaped up into the soot-smudged face of a tall, wiry blacksmith.

"But . . ." she managed to blurt, "but I'm not your wife."

"Don't ye be starting with that. We've been through this afore, ain't we? Now, stop shaming us and get ye home."

She glanced at the Highlander, who was looking on with surprise at what he surely must see as a mistake unfolding before him. The three children continued to tug on Clare's skirts and cloak, crying out and making demands. The man claiming to be her husband was wearing a heavy leather apron, and the grip on her arm testified to his trade.

"Let me go," she cried.

Rather than releasing her, the man began to drag her away.

Elizabeth could not understand how this was happening,

but it was clear enough that she was in dire straits. She looked back in desperation at Alexander Macpherson. He was standing with his hand on the hilt of the dirk sheathed at his belt, looking at the children and villagers who were beginning to crowd around him.

"Do something, Highlander. Please! I'm not his wife."

No one seemed willing to get involved, Macpherson included. He was simply standing with a look on his face that she could not decipher.

When two of the castle's guards suddenly appeared at the edge of the throng, Elizabeth dug her feet in and cried out to them. The crowd grew silent and parted, but the men made no attempt to approach.

"Help me," she begged. "You know me. I'm one of the queen's ladies-in-waiting. Tell this man to let me go. There is something gravely amiss here."

The guards looked at each other, and Elizabeth thought they actually looked amused. Fury and indignation began to crowd out her fear. When they all got back to the castle, she'd make sure there would be hell to pay.

"Your name, lass?" one of them asked, holding his hand up to shield his eyes from the rain.

Elizabeth gaped at them. They knew her. They surely knew her. But she couldn't say her name. If she said it now, the Highlander would hear, and all would be lost.

"Clare . . . Clare Seton," she responded more quietly than she'd cried for help.

The guard looked at her and shook his head. "We saw Mistress Clare at the abbey just now. Can it be there are two of you?"

The queen assured her that the guards would be there to protect her. That they would be told of the plan. Something must have gone wrong. Had she been set up by her own friends?

26

Over the heads of the crowd, Macpherson was watching attentively, standing as still as a bronze statue. She heard laughter from some of the throng of people around her.

The smith was still holding her arm. The rain continued to pour down, battering her face. Struggling against his grip, she felt cold fear wash down her back.

Her gaze darted back to the Highlander. A look of suspicion had edged into his features. He was clearly waiting for her reply to the guard's accusation.

It was no use. The ploy hadn't worked anyway. She had to give it up. Speak the truth.

"Very well," she finally called to the two castle men. "I'm Elizabeth Hay. You know who I am. Order this man to release me."

The guards moved off before she finished speaking

"Where are you going?" she shouted. "Help me. Stop!"

The horror that came with the realization that they were not going to help her lasted only a moment. The panic that replaced it instantly turned her blood to fire.

Turning on the blacksmith, she struggled, trying to wrench her arm free.

The man's grip slipped and she fell backward, skidding along in the mud and scattering a half-dozen sheep. But there was no time for escape. The smith had a hold on her again before she could even get her feet under her.

When he pulled her upright, Elizabeth saw that the road had erupted in a brawl. The Highlander appeared to be fighting the entire village. Two brutes who'd been waiting for the trouble to start were Macpherson's primary foes, trading blows with him while village women and children swarmed around him.

The world had gone mad.

"The de'il," the blacksmith muttered, his eyes wide with panic. "What now?"

Suddenly, he was dragging her toward the river as fast as he could go, and Elizabeth realized she was getting farther and farther from the only person who could help her. Screaming for the Highlander as she fought to get free, she saw him disappear beneath the mob and the two huge men.

Her abductor stopped only when they reached a boat, tied to a stake at the edge of the flooding river. The three children pretending to be hers were gone. It was now just Elizabeth and the blacksmith, if that was truly what he was. No one would ever know what became of her.

The smith shoved her into the boat, and she sprawled in the bottom, stunned by a knock to her head as she landed. Before she could react, he'd pushed off and leaped into the boat himself.

Even as he struggled against the wind to get the oars into the locks, the fast-moving current was carrying them away from the shore and quickly downriver. The boat rocked and shuddered in the raging waters, which poured in over the sides.

Furious with herself for thinking lies and trickery would succeed, Elizabeth cursed her decision to go along with the queen's plan. What was happening was simply divine retribution. She'd been out of her mind, and she was now paying for it.

5

SHE WAS no blacksmith's wife.

The panicked woman's scream cut through the roar of the wind and shouts of the villagers keeping Alexander from getting to her. And that was exactly what they were doing. Not fighting him as much as holding him back while the sooty scoundrel dragged Elizabeth away.

And she was Elizabeth Hay. Even though they'd never met before today, she matched every description he had of her. Besides, he could easily imagine some bored court chit doing something this outrageous—pretending to be someone else just to meet him covertly.

But why they had to venture out in a gale was still a mystery.

"Help me, Highlander," she shrieked over the caterwauling and the weather.

Whatever was going on, the blacksmith was dragging her out of sight toward the river.

Enough of this.

With a roar, he tossed a clinging assortment of villagers

clear of him. One of the two bruisers in the mob came at him. Alexander's fist connected with the square jaw and the monster went down. Shoving the next attacker into the advancing crowd, he ran for it, jumping across the shafts and traces of a donkey cart and racing in the direction of Elizabeth's cries.

As the flooded bank of the river came into view, Alexander saw the boat carrying the blacksmith already out in the raging current. At first, he saw no sign of Elizabeth, but then the top of a golden head appeared above the gunwale.

The gusting rain blasted his face like needles as he ran along the water's edge. The boat was spinning out of control. The smith was clearly no waterman. They were far from shore and about to disappear around the river's bend.

Alexander knew this waterway. Looping through the low, flat land beneath the castle, it quickly grew wider between here and the Firth of Forth. Turning his back on it, he cut across the bulge of land formed by the loop of the river. Moments later, he reached the bank once again.

The boat hadn't yet come into view around the bend. Branches of trees, barrels, and whole sections of a dock or a bridge floated by. A battered coracle flipped and skidded across the surface, carried by the wind. The storm was so wild now that he couldn't even see the other riverbank. Without hesitating, he dove in and began pulling himself into the middle.

As his strong strokes carried him through the churning, wind-chopped froth of brown, Alexander realized this was yet more confirmation that she could be no one but Elizabeth. Their upcoming wedding was big news in Stirling. Someone had clearly decided to kidnap the bride, assuming that Alexander would pay handsomely to recover his future wife.

Whoever was the brilliant mastermind behind the plan obviously didn't think it through very well. After all, he was the pirate Alexander Macpherson; he was the one who demanded payments. The Black Cat of Benmore paid no one.

Swimming hard, he rose to the top of a swell just as the boat swept into view. Elizabeth was up, trying to fight her captor, but the smith shoved her back down. Her head sank below the gunwale. The craft tipped as it turned in the current, and Alexander thought for a moment it was about to swamp.

As it reached him, the boat was still moving quickly. Reaching up over the side, he grabbed the man's leather apron and toppled him into the water. The man's momentum took them both under, and the current carried them beneath the boat.

Alexander lost his grip on the man's shirt and took a solid kick to the chest, pushing him down deep in the river. The Stirling folk called this Abhainn Dubh, the Black Water, and with good reason. He could see nothing.

Kicking upward, he was ready for battle. As he broke the surface, he was next to the boat, but there was no sign of the kidnapper. Taking in air, he spun around in the water and spotted the blackguard swimming hard for the shore.

Bloody Lowlanders. No fight in them at all.

With his heart pounding in his chest, Alexander grabbed the side of the boat and started to pull himself up.

He saw the oar swinging at his head at the same time that he saw Elizabeth's dismayed face. It was too late. He heard a hard cracking sound. An instant later, the world went black.

Damnation. Disaster.

"Oh, my Lord! What have I done?"

The oar dropped into the river, and Elizabeth grabbed for the Highlander's shirt and tartan before he could slip back into the torrential waters. As she tried to pull him in, a gust of wind hammered her from behind, nearly pushing her overboard.

He was heavy. They say the dead weigh more than the living.

"Come on, Highlander," she panted. "Wake up. Don't be dead."

Elizabeth felt him slip back a little, but she wasn't about to give in. If he wasn't dead, she couldn't let him drown. Pulling, tugging, she staggered as the boat rocked madly under her feet, taking more water.

She stared in horror at the depth of the water in the bottom. They were doomed.

"Why do you have to be so damned big?"

Bracing herself, she heaved just as a wave lifted his body. Managing to get his head and his arms into the craft, she paused to catch her breath. The wind was whipping her wet hair into her eyes, and she pushed it back with one hand even as she clung to his tartan with the other. She had no idea how she could get him into the boat, and he was pulling that side dangerously low.

Macpherson groaned.

"Thank the Lord!" she gasped.

She had to save him. He'd come out into a raging river to rescue her, and this was his reward.

"I didn't mean for this to happen. I'm so sorry. Really, I am."

Reaching over him, Elizabeth took hold of his thick belt. She was starting to feel as if the heavens were beating on her. The gusts continued to batter away. She was soaked to the skin and feeling exhausted, but she couldn't think about that now. She was responsible for him. She was responsible for getting him into this mess.

"We can do this. But you must help me," she pleaded to the warrior, tugging again to no avail. "Wake up, you great ape!"

Breathing heavily, Elizabeth rested her face against his head, and she saw the swelling and the cut above his temple.

"I did that. I know I did that," she whispered in his ear. "But you're not going to let a wee bump get you down, are you? Show me some of that Highland spirit."

He groaned again and a booted ankle hiked up over the side. At the same time, the boat tipped further, and she froze as more water poured in.

"We're going to drown," she muttered. "But at least we'll do it in the safety of the boat. Keep on coming."

Reaching to help him, she grabbed hold of the kilt. The boat pitched again and the wool cloth pulled up over his legs. Sprawled across his back, Elizabeth found herself looking at a bare, muscular arse. She blinked, unable to tear her eyes away.

"No time for that," she murmured, righting herself and hauling him by the belt.

This time it worked, and Elizabeth fell backward as he rolled himself in over the side.

Unfortunately, it worked far better than she expected. His head rested like a stone on her chest, his hair in Elizabeth's face. His body covered the rest of her, pinning her down and immersing all but her face in the sloshing water at the bottom of the boat.

"Nay, Highlander. This will not do."

. . .

His head hurt. He wanted to sleep. But the troublesome sea beast had dragged him into the deep. The creature had to have a dozen hands and feet. Kicking him, squeezing him, pinching him, poking him in the ribs, tugging at his hair. He tried to get a grip on the attacking appendages, but the Kraken had too many to contain.

"Highlander!"

Someone was shouting in his ear. He couldn't answer, not until he'd tamed the fiend.

Feet. He trapped a pair of them. Hands. There were too many. He growled when the creature latched its teeth onto his ear. He lifted his head and forced his eyes open.

He was nose-to-nose with a woman.

"At last!" she yelled into his face. "We're drowning. We need to get off this boat. Oh, Lord. Focus your eyes."

The small boat, the woman, how he'd come to be here— it all came back to him in a rush. The troublesome creature of his dream was no Kraken. It was Elizabeth.

"Please tell me that you're awake."

His head was pounding. Why did she insist on yelling?

"Quiet, lass," he barked, matching the sharpness of her tone. "I wasn't asleep. You took an oar to my head."

"I didn't know it was you."

Before he could respond, her face sank back beneath the surface of sloshing water. She came up a moment later, sputtering and butting him in the forehead. He thought his brain was about to explode.

"Are you trying to knock me out again?"

"Nonsense, you ignorant beast. I'm drowning."

Drowning? Everything around him was still foggy. He blinked, repeating what she'd said.

Of course. They were still in the boat. The two of them were sprawled in the bottom, and she was trapped beneath him, working hard just to keep her face above water. The blasted thing was nearly full of water.

It would only take one more powerful wave. Then the craft would go to the bottom, and they'd be left floating in the river.

"Where are we?" He pushed himself back onto his knees. "How long was I out?"

She sat up, clutching the edges as he looked around. A gust of rain slapped him in the face. They were in the middle of a full-blown tempest.

"I don't know," she replied, trying to pull her legs out from beneath him. "I was too busy saving your life to pay any attention."

Once they were out of this mess, he'd have a few things to lecture her on, starting with that point.

Alexander squinted toward the river's edge on either side. The river had widened out considerably, though with the sheets of rain and near darkness, it was difficult to see exactly how far they were from either bank. The wind was howling, kicking up waves and threatening to send them under at any moment. They had to be below the abbey, but how far was hard to say.

"Where are the blasted oars?" he demanded, looking around him.

"It was them or you," she replied over the wind. "I decided to keep you."

Perhaps he'd not be too harsh in his lecture.

They struck some half-submerged timber, and the current shoved the boat sideways. That was all it took. They swamped, and Alexander grabbed her arm.

"Swim ashore," he ordered. He pointed to what appeared to be the riverbank.

He had no opportunity to say anything more. The boat

sank beneath them, disappearing in the black water and leaving him kicking to keep his head above the surface. Fighting the current, he looked for her. She was nowhere to be seen.

"Elizabeth," he shouted as her head popped up a few yards away. As quickly as she appeared, she went under again.

Swimming hard, he closed the distance. She surfaced, her arms flailing as he reached her. When she started to go down again, he grabbed the back of her cloak and drew her up.

Gasping for breath, she wrapped her arms around his neck. She was digging her feet into his thighs, trying to climb his body.

"Go easy, lass. Float with the current," he ordered, trying to loosen her death grip on him.

"I don't know how to float," she cried, holding even tighter. "I can't swim!"

Of course. What need would a pampered royal castle dweller have for so basic a survival skill?

A wave washed over them, pushing both their heads underwater. She was practically sitting on his shoulders by the time he managed to fight his way to the surface. Spinning her in the water, he threw his arm across her chest. As he began kicking for the shore, she continued to fight him. But from the diminished depth of the scratches she was carving into his arm, he knew she was beginning to tire.

"I have you, Elizabeth," he said in her ear. "Trust me."

She heard him and stopped fighting. Turning her head, she looked over her shoulder at him. For a brief moment, their gazes locked. Her face had taken on an ashen hue; her lips were blue and trembling. Her body was still locked in a spasm of fear.

"I promise. I won't let you drown," he said.

He felt her begin to relax against him, letting him support her.

A curtain of rain and wind-whipped waves surrounded them, but Alexander did his best to keep the water from washing over her face and adding to her fright. Avoiding debris, he swam in the direction of land, or what should have been land.

They moved across the current that was carrying them quickly downriver. All he could see was brown choppy water flowing over what should have been fields.

After two days of hard rain and then this tempest, the flooding river had widened past its normal bank. Forests beyond were merely a murky black blotch in the gray-green light. He could see nothing of the pine-covered mountain ridge to the north.

His boots touched the bottom, but the current was still strong in the shallower water. He was in thigh-deep water before he judged it was safe to release Elizabeth. Her eyes were wide as she took in the landscape around them. The wind—even stronger now—pummeled them, and Alexander held her hand as they waded through the moving lake of water toward the black forests and higher ground.

Daylight was fading fast, but even in the stormy twilight, nearly everything was inundated for as far as Alexander could see. In the distance, he could make out the crown of a brae, standing like a tiny island against the flooded meadows.

"This isn't easy travel. You're doing well," he encouraged.

"Thank you for not taking my head off."

"We'll have time for that later," he said, looking ahead and pretending to ignore the look she sent him.

"I apologize for lying about my name."

Alexander glanced at her. Her cloak streamed out on the

current. The green dress was ruined, black with water and mud. The braid had come loose and her hair whipped around her in the wind. The woman was a mess. Far different from the flawless beauty who'd come through the tavern door not so many hours ago. And still, despite everything she'd endured already, Elizabeth was showing a toughness he would never have expected.

"I am also sorry for not receiving your messenger," she continued.

He didn't want to think about any of this now. His priority lay in finding shelter. He pushed on. The ground beneath the fast-moving flood was soft and treacherous. They were both slipping and fighting to keep their heads above water. By the time they reached the protruding hill, the light was gone and she was dragging. Rushing water was piling up against a boulder at the base of the hill. Holding on to it, he helped her up onto solid land.

"And I apologize for splitting your head open with the oar."

He had to give her credit for that one. She swung that wood as well as any Highland lass could have done.

Together they made their way up the slope. Shielding his eyes against the wind, he looked around him to get his bearings. He could see nothing of the countryside that he knew had fallen victim to the encroaching river. The storm showed no sign of easing. Alexander wondered if this refuge would be covered by the rising river before morning.

A thatched roof appeared beneath the crown of the hill. They nearly stumbled against it before they even saw it. It was a sheepcote with three crumbling turf walls and a thatched roof that had caved in long ago.

Elizabeth sank onto a block of stone outside one corner of the building. "Is there anything I have forgotten to apologize for?"

Alexander crouched down and felt around the area along a side wall where the roof still provided a little protection. The corner was small, but large enough for the two of them, relatively dry, and out of the wind.

"Well, do you have anything to say?" she asked, standing up when he came out.

"Aye." He took her hand and led her to the entrance of the hovel. "Welcome to your new castle."

⚜ 6 ⚜

IF ONLY HE knew how she now perceived the Highlands and the Macpherson's ancestral home after all her travels.

"Aye, m'lady," he said. "Welcome to your future."

Oh, Lord. Perhaps he did know.

Still, Elizabeth didn't need any prodding to get in out of the raging tempest. The place smelled of sheep, which was curiously comforting. As she sat in the dry corner, however, her sense of relief at being out of the wind and rain quickly gave way to misgivings about their predicament. The plan, as poorly conceived as it was, could not have gone more wrong. She was trapped now in the middle of a flood with her Highlander, pirate, rescuer, and soon-to-be husband. The two of them, alone on an isolated mound of mud. Her reputation was ruined. France was gone. Her dreams of independence were lost. Elizabeth wished she could believe in one shred of the happily-ever-after that Queen Margaret imagined.

She frowned, watching Alexander pull down handfuls of thatch and wood battens from their roof. She remained silent, realizing he was attempting to start a fire.

Even though it was midsummer, she was chilled to the bone. Water was dripping from her chin and nose, and every bit of clothing on her was soaked and filthy. She pushed the hair out of her face and stared, fascinated by her future husband.

He was crouched by the opening of the sheepcote. As he worked, drawing sparks from a flint with his dirk, the wet shirt stretched across the bulk of his muscles, molding to his broad chest and shoulders like a second skin. His hair had come loose and draped down his back. The kilt hung heavy around his legs. She knew those legs were all muscle and sinew: hard, sculpted, powerful. Elizabeth's gaze was uncontrollably drawn to them anytime he crouched. Her mouth went dry. The marriage bed would be the least of her hardships. And his face. His face.

Shite and hellfire. He was watching her inspect him.

"You're shivering so hard, lass, your teeth are going to fall out."

She tried to keep her teeth from chattering, without success, and emptied her mind of all images of his body. Also without success. She kept her eyes on the tiny flames he was urging to life. Considering the open end of the building and occasional blasts of wet wind swirling through, she didn't hold out hope that his efforts would do much to warm her up. He didn't seem affected by any of it.

Just a normal day in the Highlands.

"Take your clothes off. You'll be warmer naked than wearing all those wet things."

Naked. Images of the two of them naked—for warmth —made delicious heat rush into her belly. Oh no, that wasn't happening.

"I'm perfectly warm." She pressed her back against the wall. To prove it, she took off her cloak and laid it over her drawn-up knees. It only worsened the miserable dampness.

He broke up one of the pieces of wood into slivers and added it to the fire. As he blew on the tiny flame, Elizabeth shivered and pulled the garment up to her chin. Hopeless. She'd die of a chill before the night was over.

She froze as something crawled onto her shoulder. Wind, rain, and death by chill were instantly forgotten. Her body caught fire. She knew what it was before she saw it out of the corner of her eye. A snake.

Not just a small snake. A monster. Long and brown, its eyes glistened. A black tongue shot out and its head swayed threateningly. An adder. She was a dead woman!

Elizabeth leaped up and away from the wall, screaming. It was still on her shoulder, its tail wrapping around her neck, its demonic eyes looking into her face.

She pushed at the creature's head as she threw herself at Alexander, who was standing now by the fire. Before she could reach him, the adder dove toward her neck and found an opening above the collar. Its head disappeared and the rest was quickly following. She screeched and tore at the neckline of her dress, ripping open the stitches. Blinded with terror, she yanked and pulled, fighting her clothes.

Alexander had her by the shoulders. "What's wrong?"

"An adder," she screamed. "In my dress! Get it out!"

Grabbing the neckline in both hands, he tore the garment open with a single motion and shoved it down her arms.

The adder had found the top of her shift and was quickly moving down between her breasts.

"Be still. Let me get it."

She couldn't. She was spinning and jumping, trying to shake the creature free. The Highlander's hand went down the front of her shift, and she felt his arm against her breasts. And then, the monster was gone.

"I have it," Alexander told her. "Calm yourself. You're fine."

She opened her eyes and stared down at her exposed breasts. It was gone. It was really gone. He was holding the snake by the head, and she saw it wrap its body around his arm like a whip.

Elizabeth pulled up the shift to cover herself. Her body shook violently.

"It's not an adder." He brought the vile creature closer.

"Don't," she shrieked, stepping back. But her back immediately hit the wall, and she turned around, certain she was about to be attacked by a dozen other snakes. She had nowhere to go. No place to escape to. She'd never been so near a snake. Perhaps there were more of them already on her! Slapping at her skirts, she tried to pull the dress back up. The entire front was torn open. She held it closed over her chest.

"Since you live here," he was saying, "you should learn the difference."

"I don't live with snakes or sheep." She sounded shrill, but that was only natural under the circumstances.

"You live in Stirling. You can't lock yourself behind palace walls."

"I don't lock myself behind anything. And this is not a stroll in the gardens. This is the country. And I hate the country."

"Look at the blasted thing. It can't hurt you, lass."

"This is madness. Everyone knows an adder can kill you."

"I tell you it's not an adder."

The Highlander was holding the snake up, but he wasn't bringing it any closer. The creature was wrapped around his wrist. Clearly, he wasn't going to get rid of this killer until she paid attention.

Even as she forced herself to look, Elizabeth had to admit that he'd been quite heroic coming so immediately to her rescue. Twice now, on the river and now here.

"So what is it then?"

"A slow-worm."

She looked at the size of it. It was at least twice the length of her arm. She'd felt it trying to encircle her waist.

"That is no worm."

"A slow-worm," he said again. "It can't hurt you, but you were right to be afraid. And you were right to be thinking it was an adder. Unless a person got a good look at it, anyone might make the same mistake."

Unexpectedly, a sense of warmth flowed through her. The Highlander was not ridiculing her for the way she'd responded. She looked up into his eyes, beautiful and serious in the fading light.

"So how can you tell one from the other?"

He brought it closer. This time, the urge to run screaming out of the hovel was not entirely overwhelming.

"He has none of the adder marks on his back," he explained. "You see? He has a dark stripe, no black lightning. He can still give you a good bite, but he's not poisonous."

She looked over her shoulder, still wondering if there were more of them. "What is he doing here?"

"Trying to get out of the rain, like us."

Elizabeth shuddered, sure now there would be more unwanted visitors. The Highlander went outside and heaved the snake down the hill.

"Why did you do that?" she asked, feeling relieved but, at the same time, oddly sorry for the thing.

"It was you or him. I chose you."

The pirate charm. All the talk was true.

Alexander went back to poking at the struggling fire,

and Elizabeth looked down at the revealing rents in her dress. He'd handled her breasts in fetching the snake, but not once had she seen him leer at her or comment on it.

She clutched the dress over her chest and shivered. She was really cold, but she doubted the muddy wet cloak at her feet would offer any warmth.

"How long do you think the storm will last?" she asked as he rose to his feet.

"No way to tell. I've seen gales like this take days to blow themselves out. It must have been terrible for the folk inland."

"What do you mean?"

"All this water came from upriver. And even if the rain stops now, the flooding could get worse before it recedes. And that's not even taking into account the tide."

Elizabeth considered that. What it all meant was that she and the Highlander were going to spend some time together. Perhaps Nature was giving her the opportunity that she'd lost back at the village. No more pretending. No more lies. Now she had a chance to reason with him, to show him that she'd never make him a good wife. This was her chance to get him to release her from the marriage contract. And her reputation be damned. Enough people witnessed how she'd been caught up in this quandary.

Piling a few more pieces of splintered wood on the fire, Alexander moved to her dry corner and sat down on the packed dirt floor. Leaning his back against the wall, he kicked off his boots and stretched out his long, muscular legs. She forced herself not to stare.

"Come and sit." He patted the ground next to him. "I promise to keep you safe from snakes and any other vermin."

"I'm fine where I am," she replied, not trusting herself. Her voice had taken on a husky tone.

The night sky outside had developed a strange hue. It was brighter than the blackness of a moonless night. Still, even with the light given off by the flickering tongues of flame, it was difficult to see his face.

Elizabeth suddenly felt the need to talk. If she was going to make good use of this time together, she needed to correct any misunderstandings now.

"I want to explain why I came to you at the tavern," she began. "Why I pretended to be Clare Seton."

His gaze was fixed on the fire.

"It was a foolish plan, I know that now. But . . . but the idea was to make you see Clare and her intended and think she was me and . . . and to make you believe that my heart belonged to someone else."

He looked up at her. "Why? What did you hope to accomplish?" His tone was civil, but his expression was indecipherable.

"I wanted you to walk away from our marriage bargain."

"What was wrong with meeting me in person? Why couldn't you simply tell me?"

Reason. Of course, that would have been the logical thing to do. But how could she explain to him that such a thing took courage and at the time she didn't trust him to initiate the break? That the stakes were so high and she wasn't thinking straight?

"I should have," she said finally. "That would have been the wiser course of action. I don't want to marry you."

There. It was out. She'd told him the truth. At least, part of it. She didn't tell him about not wanting to defy her father, about the future she imagined for herself. He was staring again at the fire. She studied his face. There was no change in the relaxed way that he sat against the wall.

He glanced up at her, and something in his expression told Elizabeth that the man was relieved.

"Then . . . you're fine with this?"

His eyes sparkled in the dark.

"Aye," he said, lifting a knee and resting an arm on it. "Why do you think I was so impatient to see you these past two days? I even sent a letter to you with my squire this afternoon. He passed you with it when you came into the tavern."

"What did the letter say?" she asked, wanting him to say it. She didn't want to assume anything.

"I feel no sense of duty toward the agreement binding us together. That deal was made decades ago, and both families have already profited from it. And in return for my freedom, I'll provide a sizable sum of gold for you to do with as you please."

"You don't want to marry me?"

"Blast me if I do. You don't want to marry me, and I don't want to marry you either," he responded, looking like he'd just won the prize pig at the fair. "You can choose anyone you please, so long as it's not Alexander Macpherson."

7

IF THIS WERE A *CEILIDH*, Alexander was happy enough to lead Elizabeth in a dance that she'd need a fortnight to recover from.

A moment later, however, his enthusiasm began to wane. She stared at the fire, and he thought perhaps he'd been too abrupt telling her the truth.

Perhaps it was the timing. For five years now, Elizabeth had been of marriageable age. But he'd put off going after her. He'd found so many excuses to postpone doing what was expected of him. The fact that he was a Highlander and she a Lowlander was only the beginning of the chasm that separated them. Their traditions, their upbringing, the lives they'd chosen, all set the two of them worlds apart. He knew of too many Highland lairds whom the king had forced into political marriages with Lowland court women. And none of them seemed the happier for it. His betrothal to Elizabeth had been arranged by their family, but she'd been reared like the rest of them.

Odd that the Spey River just below Benmore Castle had

been rushing with the spring floods as well, when the Macpherson clan elders had come to speak with him about marriage. As laird, Alexander was expected to produce heirs. He knew what they wanted, but he had no wish to bring an ill-chosen spouse into their midst. And with her courtly upbringing and expectations of luxury, he was certain Elizabeth Hay would never do. Contract or no, the time had come to set the woman free. And so he'd come to Stirling.

Alexander watched her go to the threshold of the sheep-cote with her cloak and shake it ferociously. He told himself that he should be happy. The matter was resolved, and far more easily than he'd expected. As soon as this blasted storm was over, he'd take her back to her life in the queen's company, finish his other business, and be on his way.

There were plenty of fine lasses in the Highlands. Far more suitable ones.

She lifted her face to the unrelenting rain and wind, and Alexander found himself admiring her parted lips, the beautiful lines of her neck. She held the cloak to her chest and he remembered the feel of her silky skin, the fullness of her breasts as he'd pulled that lucky slow-worm from her shift.

Elizabeth was a striking woman. He couldn't argue that.

Still, irritation niggled at him. She'd attempted to deceive him, to trick him into walking away from the wedding.

Don't be a fool, he told himself. He wanted to break the contract as much as she did.

But why should she want to break the agreement? He had a great deal to offer. And it wasn't only his name and his wealth. Women thought him attractive enough. Blast him if there wasn't a chieftain's daughter in the Highlands who wouldn't gladly come to his bed if he winked at them.

But Elizabeth was no Highlander.

By the devil, he'd torn the front of her dress wide open and not taken her to bed. Her glorious breasts, the dark tips, tilting, begging to be tasted. It had taken a great deal of control to keep his eyes on her face and not on her chest. He'd wanted to toss the worm all the way to Peebles and then come back and press his lips to every curve. What would she do if he licked the salt of the river off every inch of her silky skin? His thoughts about sex, his body's immediate response to her, had come on too fast.

As she rolled up her cloak and came back in, a bundle of thatch lifted and blew away, leaving a gaping hole overhead. He hoped the roof would survive the storm. He worried about her. She'd been through a lot already. She didn't need to spend the night in the rain.

She stood looking down at the tiny fire. He decided he needed to add more pieces of the broken battens if the flames were to give off any heat. Maybe she would even take off her dress and let it dry. As he began to get up, Elizabeth picked up a handful of thatch and put it on top. Immediately, the fire sizzled and went out.

She looked at him, alarmed, recognizing her mistake.

"Oh my Lord, I smothered it. Can you start it again?"

It was an innocent mistake. But there was a skittishness about her. He wondered if he was having the same effect on her as she was having on him.

"It's no use. Everything is too wet." He patted the dirt next to him. "This is the only dry place."

She walked to the opposite corner of the hut and felt the ground. She seemed determined to be contrary. He frowned. Not a trait he allowed on his ships. Or maybe she was trying to keep her distance. She should know his intentions by now. He wouldn't take advantage of her if he wasn't to marry her.

She reached up to test the roof above her, and a section of it tumbled down on her head.

"Damnation," she cursed, jumping back and spitting out dirt and thatch.

Served her right. Alexander remained silent, watching in amusement as she brushed off her dress and hair, stamping the ground around her for fear of some creature coming down with the rest. Her cloak lay forgotten at her feet. Despite himself, his eyes lingered admiringly on the front of her dress, torn and hanging open in front. Her gaze caught his as she turned away to gather it. He knew. She remembered what he'd done for her. What his hands had touched.

He looked up as a gust of wind blasted the building, threatening to tear away what little protection they had left. She picked up the cloak and hurried to where he sat.

"The storm is not easing, is it?"

Alexander didn't answer, nor did he repeat his invitation to sit. She remained standing near him, and he could see her shivering badly. She was sure to get a chill before the night was through.

Something dropped on her head, and she fell to her knees beside him.

"What is it?" she cried, batting at her hair. "Please! Get it off of me."

He ran his hand over her wet hair and brushed away the piece of straw. He breathed in the smell of rain and earth and woman. Don't be a fool, he told himself again.

"What was it?" she asked, straightening up.

He stared at her trembling lips.

"You don't want to know."

He took her hand in his. It was ice cold.

"Give me the other one," he ordered.

For the first time, she didn't complain and did as she was told.

"How could you possibly be so warm?" she asked.

Settling down next to him, their shoulders barely touching, she let him rub her hands between his. Her fingers were long and elegant.

"Who is she?" Elizabeth stared at their joined hands. "The woman you're planning to marry?"

"There is no woman right now," he replied. "I wanted to end the agreement between us before deciding on someone else."

He paused but didn't let go of her hands.

"But I'll have to choose one soon. I have a responsibility to my clan."

"Why did you wait so long?"

Alexander wasn't going to pretend he didn't understand what she was asking. The age one married was much more important a matter for a woman than a man. And he should have acted sooner.

"I was hoping you'd choose to marry someone else," he admitted. "Decide on a husband from among the men in your circle. Courtiers and knights. Serving Queen Margaret, you must have a constant line of suitors."

The words had sounded reasonable a month ago, but now they left a sour taste in his mouth.

She made a sound that resembled a snort. "And that way, you wouldn't have to offer a settlement."

"You have no reason to think so ill of me," he protested. "I was and I am still planning to provide for you."

She rolled her eyes and pulled her hands away, leaning back against the turf wall. It wasn't about the money. She'd been well provided for. He'd done her wrong to wait this long. She'd had a right to be set free sooner. He was happy that she didn't move away.

"Why not send a letter before?" she continued. "Or a

representative from your clan? Why did you come to Stirling without telling me your plans? Everyone is preparing for a wedding."

He should have done all that, and long ago. But he hadn't. Alexander looked at her upturned face. At the direct gaze. At the perfect symmetry of eyes accented by her high cheekbones. Rumors of her beauty had reached him over the years. He had to admit that part of his reason for not releasing her was his vanity. It made him proud that others knew she belonged to him. But there was also his own prejudice regarding what he imagined to be her upbringing.

That was why he'd come. To see for himself. But her refusal to meet with him—not to even accept a message from his squire—had affirmed his decision.

"I felt I needed to explain in person," he told her, unwilling to share all that was in his mind, especially now that he knew how she felt. "And you? You could have sent an emissary or a letter."

"I couldn't openly defy my family's wishes. And besides, you know as well as I that most bridegrooms would have taken offense at such a rejection. That wouldn't have made for a comfortable way to begin a marriage, I shouldn't think."

She drew her knees to her chest, and they sat in silence for a while. She was shivering and Alexander fought the urge to gather her to his side and warm her with his own body. He was the one to speak first.

"I assume that part of your ruse regarding Clare Seton and Sir Robert Johnstone is true."

She nodded. "Aye. They're to be wed at the end of summer."

He hesitated but then decided to ask the question that kept edging into his mind.

"Is there someone else that you have set your eyes on?"

"No one," she admitted, sounding surprised. "Because our impending union was well known, no one has sought my hand. What Scot would risk drawing the wrath of the Black Cat of Benmore on himself? And frankly, I can't see such a thing happening now."

Now it was Alexander's turn to be surprised. How else could he describe the strange sense of relief he felt at her words? But at the same time, he would want her to marry, if she chose to.

"Then what did you have against our marrying?" he asked, despite himself.

She rested her chin on her knees and stared out at the driving rain. He needed to know. He refused to doubt his decision. Going their separate ways was easier for both of them.

"Say what's on your mind," he encouraged. "This may be our only chance to clear the air and walk away free people."

"I was afraid," she told him.

He frowned. "Afraid of me?"

"Not of you." She met his gaze and held it. "I was afraid of the change in my life. I am three and twenty and accustomed to the independence I have, to go and do as I wish. I cherish the comfort and freedom that I would lose."

The comfort of court life. He couldn't give her that in the north.

"Of course, I was afraid of your reputation as a pirate, as well. I imagined you to be a hard man. But I was also afraid of your people. I thought of my future as an unwelcome stranger. I know nothing of where you live in the Highlands. I could only imagine my life alone at Benmore Castle, surrounded by hostility, while you sail the seas . . . and perhaps die an early death doing it. What would be my fate then?" She shook her head.

Although this was a reputation he reveled in, her words hurt. For decades, the men in her family had seen fit to entrust Elizabeth's future in his hands, pirate or no. But she didn't share that trust. She didn't think he was capable of providing for her, protecting her—now or in the future.

And she knew nothing about the Macphersons, the kindly folk who'd been waiting for decades to welcome Elizabeth to their midst. They knew the rising fortunes of their clan had been founded upon the exchange made with Ambrose Hay's father. They were eager to accept her on that alone. She clearly had no idea that Benmore Castle was one of the great fortresses of the Highlands. Not modern, to be sure, but still a place that Alexander took pride in. And rightly so.

Whatever he did, however easy he could make her life in the Highlands, in her mind it would never match the elegance that she'd known.

"You were afraid you'd be marrying a barbarian," he said curtly.

"I didn't say that."

"You said enough."

Alexander couldn't hide the tone of disappointment in his voice. This is exactly what he'd feared. Exactly what he'd heard from those lairds who'd ruined their lives with women of Elizabeth's upbringing.

"But you've not said what you have against me," she reminded him, in the same sharp tone. "Why didn't you want to marry me?"

The bluntness of her words had torn down the curtain of courtesy. Alexander knew he had to say what was on his mind or he'd forever regret not speaking.

"I didn't want to marry you because I knew you'd be unsuitable as a wife."

"Unsuitable?" she repeated, her eyes rounding in protest.

"I knew you'd be unprepared for Benmore Castle," he asserted. "You've lived your entire life in court. I doubted you'd be capable of adjusting to our ways."

"You think I'm spoiled and weak."

"I didn't say that."

"You said enough."

🥀 8 🥀

THE LONG, sustained creak that invaded her dream exploded with a loud crack just before a swirling gust of rain drenched her.

"Oh my Lord!"

Elizabeth sat up, groggy and unfocused. The portion of thatched roof above her was gone and the rain was pouring down. As she skittered to the side, she realized she was alone.

"Alexander?"

There was no answer. He was gone. But he couldn't be. He dove into a raging flood to save her. He'd never leave her alone like this. Where was he?

"Shite, shite, shite."

Awake now and fighting back panic, she looked around the sheepcote. He couldn't have left without her.

Grey daylight filled the open wall of the hovel. Staring out at the storm, she had no idea what time of day it was. She glanced up as the wind buffeted her and then wrenched away another section of the roof. The place was coming

MAY MCGOLDRICK

apart with each gust of the wind. Where was the
Highlander?

"Please don't let this be happening."

Elizabeth tried to remember to breathe as she jumped
to her feet. Last night, they'd exchanged words. Each of
them had insulted the other when they should have held
their tongues. She couldn't have offended him so much that
he'd clear out without so much as a word.

He was made of the hardier stock than that. He deliv-
ered verbal punches as easily as he took them. He wouldn't
desert her unless something had gone wrong. Or perhaps
he'd gone for help. But why not wake her, tell her?

"Damnation."

She was cold. Her cloak was in a protected corner,
dangling from a rudely fashioned hook. She didn't recall
hanging it up. She poked at it, making sure no vermin had
taken possession, before pulling it down.

She was still wet—or wet again from the wake-up
drenching—but at least she'd slept. The storm howled
around them all night. But every time she stirred, the
warmth behind her had lulled her back to sleep.

She paused, trying to decide if the warmth was a dream
or real. She recalled snuggling into it, unable to get close
enough.

Wind, saturated with rain, swept through the hut, and
Elizabeth threw the cloak around her shoulders. Pulling up
the hood, she fastened the ties and went out. Her heart
sank.

"Disaster," she murmured.

A chill clutched at her insides. The flood had risen
overnight. It was now a few yards below the sheepcote. The
surface of the moving waters was littered with trees and
shrubs and half-submerged timber from bridges and farms
and Lord knows where.

She didn't want to think or imagine that something could have happened to him. What happened if he tried to swim through this to get help? What if he drowned?

This was all her fault. She shouldn't have bought into Queen Margaret and Clare's plan, to begin with. But it was her fault. The stupid notion of playing games. Her cowardice in not meeting with him and telling him the truth. Life was not a few steps in a dance or a promenade in a masque. She'd endangered a man's life. Tears welled up in her eyes. She couldn't live with herself if something happened to him.

Worry for Alexander wrenched her gut as she turned to go around the building. The wind whipped her hood over her face, and she banged directly into a broad, muscular chest.

Her heart leaped with joy. She looked up, overwhelmed with relief. Her fists struck him on the chest to make sure he was real.

"You came back for me."

He looked down at her and smiled. "I didn't go anywhere."

Whatever words were said in the heat of the moment last night, they meant nothing to her now. He was safe. He was here. Her eyes took in the wet shirt clinging to his chest. Her fists opened, and she let herself feel the strong beat of his heart. She wanted to throw her arms around his neck and kiss him. He was safe. Safe.

He reached out and laid a warm palm on her forehead.

"Are you unwell?" he asked. "Feeling feverish?"

Elizabeth realized she was smiling like a fool.

"Nay, I'm perfectly well. How is that wound on your head?"

"It was barely a scratch."

Elizabeth's insides quivered and began to melt as he

peeled a wet twist of hair off her cheek and tucked it behind her ear. His fingers traced her sensitive lobe, the line of her jaw, trailing down her throat before they slowly fell away. His touch played havoc with her senses.

The memories of last night rushed back. Following their quarrel, Elizabeth had curled up in the dirt with the smell of dampness and animals around her. The tense silence had been as chill as the wind, but she'd finally fallen, shivering and exhausted, into a restless half-sleep. Looking at him now, she knew the source of that enveloping warmth. It was no dream. Alexander lying down behind her, his powerful arm drawing her in against him. His thumb ever so often softly caressing a band of exposed skin beneath her breasts. Dream or no dream, she'd made no objection. In fact, she'd wanted more. She'd wanted him to move his hand and touch the tips of her aching breasts.

Rain continued to pelt down on them, but neither moved. Her mouth was dry, her heart pounded madly against her ribs. Elizabeth couldn't understand what was happening to her. She wondered if he remembered last night, too.

She lifted her gaze. He truly was a beautiful man. In this strange light, his eyes were the darkest shade of blue. They were the color of the morning sky at dawn. Strands of his long hair had escaped the tie and hung about his sculpted face. She almost reached up and tucked the locks behind his ear, but she didn't trust herself. Even now her palms tingled from the feel of his chest.

A sharp gust of the wind blasted them, and the building groaned precariously.

"We have to go," he said.

She was relieved and disappointed that the spell was broken. Elizabeth followed him as he turned and walked around toward the rear of the building.

"We need to move north, away from the river," he said over the wind. "To that line of forests."

Alexander was all business now. The gentle hand that had just caressed her face was pointing at the vague blotchy line of black in the distance.

"There's no easy way to get there," he told her. "It's all flooded."

Her stomach clenched with worry. Their situation was grimmer than she could have possibly imagined. They were at the top of a brae that would soon be inundated. She stared at the moving sea that two days ago had been meadow and farmland.

"We can't stay here," he added. "The water will get deeper the longer we tarry."

She recalled her struggles in the river, thinking every breath would be her last. Helpless, drowning, her body sinking like a millstone no matter what her arms tried to do. She felt her heart racing. She really didn't want to go back in that water.

"How deep do you think it is?"

He shrugged. "These lands along the river are fairly flat, but there are bound to be some gullies."

Deep breaths would not ease the sour taste of calamity rising in her throat. But she had to do it. They had no choice. Elizabeth started down the hill. With each step she took, her feet sank into the saturated ground, and her dress and cloak gained extra layers of muck. Before they were halfway to the water, her progress abruptly halted when one foot wouldn't come out.

"Is this your first time wandering down a hillside in inclement weather?" his voice teased.

He was beside her, and Elizabeth had a feeling he was entertained by her misery. So they were going to play this game again. She forced her attention from the watery fate lying ahead to the man beside her. She wasn't alone. He would help her, save her.

"You call this inclement, Highlander?" she scoffed, hoping the tremor in her voice didn't betray her anxiety. "I do this every Monday and Friday. And sometimes on Wednesdays, as long as it rains."

Pulling her foot out, she nearly went headlong down the rest of the slope, but he caught her. He was with her. Alexander was with her. She kept repeating the words in her mind as they continued on. At the bottom of the hill, he stopped and pointed downriver.

"We'll go in that direction. The bogs that I remember are mostly to the west of where we came ashore."

"Bogs?" She took a step back from the water, bumping into him. Not just drowning. Disappearing. Getting swallowed up by the earth. How many more things could go wrong?

"We'll need to be careful, but we'll come through this."

He put a hand on her shoulder and squeezed gently. She knew it was meant to be a comforting gesture, but she would rather have faced a hundred snakes than this. You can run from a snake; you can't run from a drowning.

Elizabeth recalled what he'd said last night. In his eyes, she was weak, "unsuitable." Maybe she was . . . in this situation. She'd never been trapped in a flood before. But she wasn't about to complain. He was with her. He knew what to do.

"This will be a wee bit arduous for you, I know."

"I'll be fine."

He looked at her gently for a moment. His hand cupped the side of her face, his blue eyes locking with hers. "I'll be there with you."

Her silent chants had reached his mind. She trusted him.

But fear had too strong a hold on her limbs. She looked at the brown, swirling water. Two dozen steps in the shallows before she reached the waiting disaster. But she had to do it. This was a matter of honor. Courage, she told herself.

"And I'll be with you," she said. "Never forget that oar, Highlander."

He chuckled as she lifted her dress and cloak to her knees and stepped into the water. It was colder today than yesterday.

Alexander held out his hand to her. Not yet, she thought. The branches of a tree spread out on the surface not too far away. It couldn't be too deep.

"I can manage," she told him.

The next step put Elizabeth in up to her chest. Panic flooded through her as the current carried her off her feet. Her body responded as she expected. But she was not a millstone—she was the entire mill. Her head went under. Her hands touched the slimy bottom. She opened her mouth to scream, and briny water filled her mouth. Suddenly, he was right there, taking hold of her by the waist and bringing her to the surface.

She gagged and coughed up a gallon of water.

"Breathe."

She clutched at his arm, gasping for breath. He was swimming out into the current and taking her with him.

"Breathe."

"I am breathing!" she screamed into the wind once she found her voice. She felt for the bottom with her feet, but there was nothing there. Nothing to stand on. She was going to drown. They'd never reach higher ground.

She clawed at his arm, trying to hold on tighter. But it wasn't enough. Fearing he would lose his grip on her, she struggled to turn around and hold onto his neck.

"Nay, lass. That won't do. Unless you want to drown us both."

He continued to work his way along, sometimes swimming, sometimes wading.

Breathe. Breathe, she told herself. Close your eyes so you don't see the Grim Reaper coming for you. But she couldn't.

"Float beside me. Let your feet come up. I have you."

Easier said than done. She tried to float, but her feet immediately sank and her face went under. This time, he pulled her out before she could gulp down another mouthful. She tried again to float, but it was impossible.

He pulled her back in against his chest, and she clung to his arm with both hands.

"The current is nowhere as strong as what we faced yesterday."

Easy for him to say. For Elizabeth, drowning was the same—whether it happened in a river, a pond, or a baptismal font.

But drowning wasn't the worst way to die. She thought about the bogs Alexander mentioned. Even in the castle, she'd heard tales of animals and people wandering into them unawares and dying a horrible death. She'd once heard of a donkey sucked all the way to Hell before you could cross yourself.

He stepped on something and the water reached his chest. Elizabeth felt for the bottom with her feet. Nothing. Hot claws of panic continued to scratch at her. What happened if she lost her hold and they were separated? What if they were crossing a bog and the mud reached up to grab him? What if she had to save him?

She pressed herself closer to him. Moving his arm so he had a better hold on her, one palm ended up cupping her breast. It would figure, the day she was to drown or get swallowed up by a bog, a man touches her breast. And what was her reaction? Hold on tight. Please don't let me die.

"Regardless of where you've lived, lass, you're still a Scot."

He was talking. She was quivering in terror, and he was talking like they were taking a stroll in the gardens.

"What do you mean by that?" She looked over her shoulder at him.

"How is it you never learned to swim?"

Swim? Swim? He was being critical of her now? "I didn't have time for it."

"Too busy with all the court revelry, I suppose? Too much time primping and dressing and dancing, and no time for learning anything useful?"

"If you call knowing one snake from another useful, you're correct."

How wrong could he be? She'd never learned to swim because she'd had no one to teach her. And as she grew older, she'd been busy caring for her father, who in turn was always busy with his building projects. It was a fortunate thing that Ambrose Hay was constantly sought after for working on palaces and castles. It was only when she wasn't at his side that she learned polite manners by emulating the women she came in contact with.

"Probably couldn't tell a rock cod from a raspberry, unless it was served up for you."

Eager to respond, she tried to turn and gulped down a mouthful of muddy water for her trouble. Coughing and gagging and sputtering, she grabbed for him. He drew her closer, holding her against him.

"Breathe."

"I am breathing," she snapped, angry that he would find a moment like this to be disparaging of her education.

"Let me ask you this: Can you identify an ogival arch?"

"Aye, I know the man well. Archibald Ogilvie, bishop of Glasgow."

"Not Ogilvie . . . ogival! Ogives are the intersecting transverse ribs that make the surface of a vault. It is a pointed arch."

"I'm not so sure about that, lass. Archie has a pointed head, but I don't think he'd be caught dead intersecting anyone's ribs."

"Ha!" she laughed. "So there are a few things you don't know. I don't suppose you could tell a chevette from a narthex."

"Are they a kind of a song? Nay, I've got it. They're dances."

He was teasing her. She could hear it in his tone. The nerve of the man!

"And I doubt you could tell me how many columns it takes to support a domed roof. Or how many flying buttresses were needed for the cathedral at Chartres."

"Useful survival knowledge to have. I am quite impressed."

He wasn't.

"I didn't think you'd know," she concluded triumphantly. "For your information, I spent most of my time at my father's side as he built some of the most important palaces in Europe. If I didn't have time to learn to swim, it was because I was busy. So if you have something else to say . . ."

"Well, I was just going to say, I'll be happy to carry you all the way to Stirling. But I thought you might want to walk a wee bit."

Elizabeth looked around her. The rain and wind were still beating down on them, but he was standing on a strip of ground a dozen paces from the water. A pine forest rose up on one side of them, and the flood they'd just emerged from stretched out on the other.

"Put me down," she said.

"As you wish, m'lady."

"How did we get here?"

"A miracle, I think."

"You held me through it all?"

"Actually, with all the talk, I thought you and your father would construct a bridge for us, but alas it was not to be."

"You're incorrigible."

"I am."

She realized now what he'd been doing. Distracting her, making her talk to take her mind off her fears. She gazed out at the watery expanse. It was behind them. She was alive.

Alexander was striding along the water following the line of woods.

"Where are you going?" she asked. "Isn't Stirling the other way?"

"We won't make it, going that way. Not until this blasted storm stops and the waters recede. We'll head for Dunfermline and maybe find a place to dry out."

She hurried to keep up with him.

"Thank you for . . ."

The Highlander stopped short and she ran into his back.

"And just to be clear on things, a chevette is a wee chapel in a church and the narthex is the entrance. I'd need to know the height and diameter of a dome to tell you how many pillars would be needed to hold the bloody thing up. And I've never counted the buttresses at Chartres, but I'm guessing twenty-six. Am I close?"

Without waiting for an answer, Alexander turned on his heel and started off again, leaving her speechless.

Elizabeth couldn't be sure, but she thought she saw him hiding a grin as he strode away.

Devil take him, the man was marvelous.

9

ELIZABETH'S SHOCK at his response was priceless. Alexander nearly laughed, and the only way to hide it was to walk away.

Working his way along the water's edge, he heard her continue to shout at him, but he didn't want to slow down. She'd made assumptions about him, and he'd done the same. But there was an appeal in correcting her misconceptions a little at a time. They'd be traveling together for a while, anyway. Why dish out all the fun at one time?

"You wait for me," Elizabeth ordered as he started up the hill on the far side. "You have some explaining to do."

Alexander continued to climb. Even here, his boots either slipped or sank deeply. He knew the going would be even more difficult for her. Right now, that was a good thing. He needed to put some distance between them, if only to give himself time to cool the growing urge to kiss her.

Blast her, if she wasn't trouble. She was funny, smart, and—regardless of everything she'd gone through since yesterday—the woman refused to give in. She was holding her head high. He had to respect that. He'd certainly not expected such toughness in her. And then there was her mud-covered face, the tangle of hair that had once been a golden braid, the violet-blue eyes that showed the strain of cold and lack of proper sleep. She was beautiful.

And "trouble" was exactly the right word. The more time he spent with her, the more doubts he had about the decision he'd made. Perhaps he'd been too quick in judging what he thought she would be. Perhaps he should have waited and gotten to know her.

Last night, holding her trembling body in his arms, he'd tried to warm her. The problem had been his awareness of what lay beneath that torn dress, and that embrace had become more of a torture for him as the night went on. As she lay there asleep, so trusting, she had no idea of how much he wanted her. As she relaxed, she hugged his hand to her breast and he could feel the strong heart beating there.

Alexander had needed to roll away. If he hadn't, she would have awakened with a full knowledge of how aroused he was.

He'd lain awake for hours, listening to the battering winds of the storm, thinking of his ships and the ports he'd visited, picturing in his mind the crops in the Macpherson fields. He thought about whether this storm was ravaging Benmore Castle. Forcing himself to consider these other things, he was able to make his body behave. Until the next time she moved or murmured softly in her sleep.

Damn him if it wasn't the longest, most enjoyably torturous night he'd ever endured.

"Alexander Macpherson, you stop this moment," she called. "Or I swear I won't save you the next time you're flopping around my boat like a dead fish."

He considered telling her that dead fish don't flop, but he'd reached the top of the low rise. In the distance, he saw a wee thatched cottage and its outbuildings tucked in against the forest. The fields were underwater, and from what he could see the floods had reached the largest shed. But for Elizabeth's sake, he was relieved to see the cottage appeared to be safe so far. He could see no sign of life anywhere.

The woman was now cursing with the enthusiasm of a seasoned sailor. Where in court life had she learned that?

Looking back, he found her mired in the muck, one arm in up to the elbow and her feet completely buried. Working his way back down the hill and through the mud to her, he leaned over and offered her a hand.

"I don't need your help," she said. "I can manage."

Alexander stood back, watching as she pulled one arm out to only have the other one sink into the ground. Her feet were doing the same dance; one went in as one came out. He moved in to help and she looked up, her eyes blazing.

"I said I can do this."

He crossed his arms and watched until she finally managed to stand up, only to lose her balance and land on her arse.

He couldn't take seeing her suffer like this. Despite her vocal and rather alarming threats, he looped his arm around her waist, lifted her out, and put her down at the base of the rise.

"I didn't want your help," she grumbled.

Now he couldn't help but smile. There wasn't a space left on her face, her neck, arms, or cloak that wasn't covered.

"What are you grinning at?"

"You are without doubt the filthiest looking woman I've ever seen."

"And you think you look any better?"

He glanced down at his shirt and tartan. He was carrying about a bucket full of mud on each boot, to be sure, but wading and swimming through the floodwaters had washed away the worst of it from his clothes.

"I definitely look better."

Elizabeth scooped two handfuls of mud from her cloak, rubbed it on his shirt, and finished with a couple of streaks on his face. He waited silently until she was finished, every nerve in his body telling him to take her in his arms and find her lips beneath that mess.

Happy with her efforts, she smiled brightly, her cobalt blue eyes meeting his.

"Now you look better," she said, stepping around him.

He took a deep breath and shook his head in amusement. He stayed a few steps behind as she made her way up the rise, ready to help if she fell again. Blast her. This was not the Elizabeth Hay he'd imagined. That botched kidnapping was the best thing that could have possibly happened to them. He lifted his face to the wind and the stinging rain. This bloody storm was the best thing that could have happened to them.

And the worst.

"We're saved," she called back excitedly, reaching the top of the hill. "A farm. A building with a roof. People."

He didn't want to disappoint her about the last part. They might indeed find someone huddled in the cottage, but it looked more like whoever lived there had either left as the flood waters rose, or had been away from the farm when the storm struck. When they were an arrow shot from the buildings, he stopped her.

"Wait here," he ordered. "I'll go first and warn the farmer before you show yourself."

"Very funny," she retorted.

Alexander didn't expect any hostility from the cotter,

arriving as they were during stormy weather, but he wanted to be safe. Despite the river of water running between the cottage and the sheds, the farm was organized and well-kept.

At the door, he called out a greeting but got no answer. Pushing it open, he ducked his head and went in.

As he expected, the place was empty. A cooking fire against one wall was cold, but dry wood had been stacked in the corner. A roughly made table and two blocks of wood that served as stools sat nearby. A spinning wheel and a small hand loom. Overhead, braided bunches of herbs hung from the low rafters. At the opposite end of the room, there was a straw mattress on a rude bed, and a chest of unfinished wood. Opening the top of the chest, he saw neatly folded clothing.

Alexander decided that the folk living here were only away because of the floods. They'd left their belongings behind. But he was equally sure that leaving them some coins when he and Elizabeth moved on would be appreciated.

When he went out to call for Elizabeth, she was standing by the door, a stout stick of firewood in her hands.

"I told you to wait."

"I did. I waited. But you took so long that I was worried someone might have cut your throat. I came to rescue you . . . again." She dropped the stick and looked past him into the hut. "This will definitely do."

He couldn't bring himself to lecture her.

Before going inside, she looked down at her muddy shoes. "I can't track all of this into someone's home."

He was going to remind her of the dirt floor in the cottage, but she'd already pulled the dress up to her knees and was trying to remove her shoes.

Alexander found himself staring at her shapely calves

and ankles, and thinking of the situation they were in. The two of them, alone in this hut for however long it took the river to recede. The rain and wind didn't show any sign of letting up, but it didn't look like the floods would reach the cottage. They'd be safe here.

She was still struggling to untie the soaked knots on her shoes when he felt his loins tighten. He tore his eyes away from her legs. He was in trouble.

Distance. And food. Those were the two things he needed most right now.

"Go inside and stay there," he told her. "I'll check the barn."

"Are you sure that—?"

"If I need saving, I'll call you."

In her entire life, Elizabeth never felt as great a need to impress someone as she was feeling now. Alexander had already upended many assumptions she'd had about him. Now she was determined to make him feel the same way. They might not have a future together, but she wanted him to realize she was not the prissy court brat he'd imagined her to be. And if he regretted not wanting her as his wife, she could live with that, too. It was a matter of pride.

Coming up to the cottage, she'd seen what looked like a kitchen garden behind it. She was thirsty and starving, but she wasn't about to mention it to him. She watched him until he made his way across the ankle-deep water running down through the farmyard and disappeared into the largest shed. Leaving her shoes on, she went around to the back of the building.

The cursed rain and wind continued to batter her as she made her way around. Weariness from the journey was catching up to her. Her sodden dress and cloak were as heavy as a knight's armor, and she was certain her skin beneath was now permanently shriveled. She half expected her limbs, one by one, to unfasten themselves and drop into the mud.

Her spirits lifted when she spotted the garden. The wicker fence of woven willow that surrounded it had been nearly destroyed, and many of the plants were flattened, but abundant green foliage held the promise of something to eat. The mud was thick between the rows. Her mood rose even higher when she also saw the line of rain barrels overflowing with clean water.

Elizabeth only realized how thirsty she was after drinking three ladles of water. He had to be thirsty, too. For a change, she'd do something for him. She'd be useful. Carry water in. Harvest some greens from the garden. This entire misadventure was due to her, and yet Alexander continued to come to her rescue. This was the chance to earn her keep.

She turned back to the garden and pulled a plant. The parsnip was of a good size. Not enough to feed a woman and a giant, but certainly a start. She reached down to pull a second one. But the root stuck. She pulled harder, with no success. And harder. The parsnip greens gave suddenly, breaking free and sending Elizabeth flying backward.

Going down, her arse landed on a soft cushion. She looked down in horror at the cone-shaped basket she was sitting on.

"Damnation."

Before she could move, angry bees were everywhere.

The partially flooded shed had been built into the side of a low hill. A handful of animals were tethered there, up and out of harm's way. A cow, three pigs, and a pair of goats barely gave him a second glance when he climbed the ladder and peered at them in the murky light. Up in the rafters, chickens eyed him with alarm. They must have sensed how hungry he was.

Alexander was not about to slaughter any of these and take food out of the mouths of the cotters. Still, he was thinking about milk and eggs when he heard quacking coming from behind the shed. Going back down, he found a flooded pond behind the building with scores of ducks. One wildfowl would barely be missed, and the payment he intended to leave would more than compensate the farmer's loss.

A few moments later, he carried their future dinner to a bench beneath an overhang facing the cottage. He wasn't naïve enough to think Elizabeth could handle plucking or cleaning the fat bird.

As he began to work, he glanced across at the farmhouse. The door was ajar, but there was no sign of smoke from the opening in the roof. He should have started the fire himself, he realized. Right now, she was probably inside, stripping off her cloak and ruined dress. He imagined Elizabeth standing there, washing the grime from her naked body, rinsing her hair and skin with a bucket of clean water, perhaps even watching him through the partially open door. Tearing his eyes away, he forced himself to focus on yanking the feathers from the duck.

Devil take him if he wasn't losing control. He wanted her. He couldn't deny it. The thought kept pushing itself to the front of his brain. And the more time they spent together, the less he could remember why he'd been against their marriage to start with.

Alexander wondered if she felt the same way about him. He'd noticed how closely she watched him. And she was quick to reply to his teasing with her own barbs. Blast him, if that wasn't another thing he liked about her. He enjoyed a woman with a sharp mind and words she wasn't shy about using. And if Elizabeth was a wee bit loud, well, he could always . . .

Loud. He focused.

She was screaming.

Dropping the half-plucked fowl on the bench, Alexander shot across the flooded farmyard, dagger in hand. Her cries were coming from behind the cottage, and he followed the sound of her voice. At the bottom end of a wrecked kitchen garden, he spotted Elizabeth standing rooted to the ground like a tree. Her cloak lay in the mud, and bees were buzzing like a cloud around her in the wind.

"Get them off of me," she cried when she saw him.

Alexander sheathed the dagger as he approached. "Another skirmish with country life?"

"Bees. They're on me. Crawling all over me."

He saw the bees were indeed on her, and he was relieved that she had enough sense to remain still. Panicked noises came from her throat, and he wondered how long it would be before she ran for it. He'd seen many a man and boy tear off like a wounded stag when a single bee buzzed about.

"Shite, shite, shite!" she moaned.

"Bees don't like the rain." He glanced at the grass-woven bee skeps in the garden. One of the baskets lay almost flattened next to her. "You tipped over their hive."

"I fell on it. Landed on it."

"And the busy wee creatures took exception to it."

"It wasn't intentional," she keened. "A parsnip tricked me."

He glanced down at the vegetables near her feet. She'd been trying to get them something to eat.

"Get them off my . . . off my face." She shut her mouth and eyes but continued to make a moaning sound.

"You're doing the right thing. Don't move," he said in what he hoped was a calm tone.

He was no expert. He was certainly no beekeeper, but he'd seen a great many people stung in his life. He'd been stung a number of times himself, but he'd also heard stories of folk dying from it. Alexander remembered as a lad seeing a priest who lived not far from Benmore working with his bees. The swarm never hurt him.

What he needed to do now was to keep Elizabeth calm while he figured out what to do. The skep she'd crushed was filled with bees and broken wax combs that were oozing honey.

The bees were on her face, crawling on her hair, but she hadn't yet been stung, apparently. Actually, that was a bloody miracle.

"Keep your mouth and eyes closed," he ordered. "I'm right here."

He spotted a battered bushel basket that the wind had jammed up into a corner of the wattle fence. Retrieving it, he stood in front of her, turning it upside down. Rain continued to pelt down.

He brought the basket closer and brushed gently at her face, trying to encourage them to fly up into this offered shelter. They were slow to move. He couldn't blame them.

Alexander worked slowly and methodically, moving across her hair, her forehead, her nose, her dripping chin. They were even on the seam of her lips. He touched her gently, brushing away the intruders. He saw tears streaming down her cheeks, mingling with the rain, but she remained steadfastly still.

"I have most of them off your face," he told her.

"My dress," she whimpered.

As he brushed the bees off her neck, his fingers caressed the silky skin. They were now following each other into the basket, out of the hard rain. It took time, and her courage was impressive. Equally impressive was his own patience, not becoming distracted by this beauty standing before him. With the exception of a few strays, most of them were off her. He propped the basket up on a rock under the hedge. She still hadn't moved.

He stared at the dress. The curves of her breast showed through the torn neckline, above the exposed shift.

"They're inside my clothes."

"Most of them are gone."

"They're crawling down inside my shift. I feel them. You need to do something."

"Inside your dress?"

"Do something," she cried.

There was nothing else he could do. There was no getting around this.

"Keep perfectly still," he ordered.

The dress already had more holes in it than a tinker's promise. The seams were torn open in a dozen places, but he took his time pulling it open at the neckline. His knuckles lay against the warm, firm flesh of her breasts, and one of the invaders crawled up onto his thumb before flying away.

Alexander was glad she still had her eyes closed or she'd be far more frightened by the reaction of his body than the bees.

As he peered down the front of her dress for others, raindrops splashed on her chest and formed sparkling rivulets on her skin. Two more bees crawled into sight and flew off toward the hedge.

"You're right. There are more," he told her. The huskiness in his voice made his words sound more like a growl. "I have to strip you down."

"Do it. Do it now."

Alexander was lost. Last night, he'd been able to exercise some control. Now, standing here in the light of day, he had no choice. He had to see what he was doing. And what his eyes saw, his body reacted to.

Devil take him, he was only a man, after all.

He gently peeled the dress down her arms and pulled it over past her hips until it dropped to the ground. The shift was wet and it hid nothing. A bloody saint would have found it impossible not to stare at the perfect roundness of her breasts or the pink tips poking through the nearly transparent material. And he was no saint.

He unfastened the ties down the front of the shift. As her body came more and more into view, he swallowed hard and tried to stifle the maddening urge to lean down and take her nipples between his lips. Making himself do what needed to be done, he pulled the shift down off her shoulders. As it clung to her hips, he shooed away the handful of insurgents beneath her breasts and on her belly. Moving around her, he drew the cloth away from the small of her back and saw a few had made their way there, working themselves down onto the curve of her buttocks. He reached down and brushed them away.

Standing there in the driving rain with her shift hanging at her hips, she was exposed to him, to his eyes, to his touch. And Elizabeth was perfection in every sense.

"I think I got them all," he said in that stranger's voice.

When he looked into her face, her eyes were open. Her gaze was fixed on him. He gently pulled the shift back up onto her shoulders. Without saying anything, she threw her arms around his neck.

He hadn't realized it, but she was still crying. He was a villain being so focused on her body and not paying attention to how frightened she'd been.

"Were you stung?"

Elizabeth shook her head and continued to shiver. Whatever words she was trying to say were lost with her face buried against his chest.

Rain continued to pound them. Her dress and cloak were lying in the mud. He lifted her in his arms and carried her around the cottage. She rested her face against him, still quivering.

Inside, Alexander sat her on the edge of the bed. Untying the laces of the muddy shoes, he gently removed them. She peeled off her stockings and stared at the blanket he held open.

"You'd be better off without those clothes."

She took a deep breath but didn't hesitate. Shrugging out of the shift, she pushed her drawers down, stepping out of them, as well.

Alexander's heart pounded in his chest. Her hair fell in wild, tangled cascades of burnished gold along her face and arms. Her body was streaked with mud, and her long shapely legs descended from curved hips that matched the fullness of her breasts. Stunned by the vision, he hesitated for a few moments longer than he should have. She took his breath away. Finally coming to his senses, he placed the coarse woolen blanket around her shoulders.

She sank down onto the straw mattress, dropped onto her side, and drew her knees to her chest. Her eyes closed.

Damn me. Damn me. Damn me, he cursed silently. He was a pirate and one who'd earned his reputation. He lived by his wits and his love of a fight and his willingness to take what he wanted. But that had never applied to women. Never in his life had he ever mistreated or taken advantage of one.

But right now, looking down at Elizabeth, her shoulder peeking out from beneath that blanket, he was wondering if he'd be able to say that before the day was out. He wanted her. He wanted to feel himself inside of her, regardless of the right or wrong of it. He'd ruined the chance of having her as his wife. She didn't belong to him.

Which meant only one thing. He had to get out.

Alexander stomped to the door. He'd left a half-plucked fowl out there somewhere.

He paused at the sound of a soft voice coming from the bed.

"I'm not weak, Highlander."

He turned and looked at her. Even in the dim light of the cottage, her eyes were bright.

"You're not weak," he agreed. "You're the bravest woman I know."

10

SHE AWOKE DRY AND WARM. Lying there, Elizabeth couldn't recall the last time she felt this way. She also didn't recall falling asleep.

Her stomach growled, and she realized it was the smell of roasting meat that roused her. As she stretched on the bed, her feet slipped out from beneath the blanket. She sat up and looked around the cottage.

"Alexander?"

There was no sign of him, but she saw the bird on an iron spit over a fire.

Alexander. She lay back again and closed her eyes. The brave Highlander who'd come to her rescue over and over again. The honorable man who'd forgiven her error in judgment and not once reminded her that they were in this predicament because of her foolish blunder. The gallant hero who'd undressed her, seen her naked, touched her flesh, but not once taken advantage of her vulnerable condition. The courteous laird who'd even prepared a meal.

Alexander. Not my Alexander. Not my Highlander. She remembered the wistful tone in Queen Margaret's words

about romance. Now she understood. Elizabeth now realized the extent of her error in judgment.

Where was he?

The crackling flames and the hiss of dripping fat were
the only sounds. No wind whistled past the edges of the
shutters or the door. No gusts of rain battered the walls of
the cottage. Was it possible that the storm was over?

Wrapping the blanket around her, she got out of bed.
He couldn't be too far away.

How had this happened? In her entire life, she'd always
been in control. She was not prone to accidents. She was
not clumsy. She'd never needed to be rescued, and here
Alexander had saved her yet again.

Recalling how she'd stood naked before him, Elizabeth
felt the heat rise and spread across her skin. But she hadn't
felt the blush of modesty then. She'd simply wanted to be
free of the bees and the wetness that had seeped into her
bones. But it was more than that. Something in her world
had shifted. Something existed now that hadn't existed
before.

Into her mind came the painting she had seen in
Florence in the palace of the Magnifico. Botticelli's vision
of Venus. With the flood waters of the sea all around her,
her golden hair flowing across her uncovered skin, the
goddess showed no false sense of modesty. She was willing
to share this intimate view of herself. Earlier, when
Alexander had gazed at her, she suddenly knew how Venus
felt.

And she wanted him. After he'd carried her back into
the cottage, she would have freely given up the blanket if
he'd have stripped off his clothes and used his body to warm
her. Skin to skin. Her hands all over his chest and back and
arms. Holding him against her, belly to belly, thigh to thigh.

She touched her flushed cheeks and tried to ignore the

wobbly knees and the heavy, tingling sensation in her breasts.

There was no sign of her undergarments or her dress or shoes. Near the bed, the wooden chest had been left open. She looked through the folded clothing. A man's shirt and breeches. A woman's woolen dress. She took it out and laid it on the bed. At the bottom of the chest, she found the partially sewn pieces of a tiny linen dress.

"You have a bairn on the way," she murmured to the absent mistress.

Replacing the baby's garment, Elizabeth glanced around the cottage. She'd overlooked the freshly sawn wood stacked in one corner beside a half-built cradle.

As she stared at it, an unexpected thought edged into her consciousness. In recent years, she'd been fighting the notion of marrying this Highlander, hostile to the thought of finding herself deserted in a place where she'd be a stranger, away from everything she knew and cared about. She'd made herself believe happiness lay in the life she had with her father. Travel, grandeur, building, learning. She'd imagined it was all or nothing. One way or the other.

She'd scoffed at thoughts of having a family of her own, of planning a future that encompassed anything beyond her own needs and desires. But here, wrapped in a coarse blanket of homespun wool, she realized this tidy cottage glowed with an aura of tenderness, of happiness that existed not despite life's toil, but because of it.

And for the first time, she longed for something like that in her own life.

The hiss of juices drew Elizabeth's attention. The duck was on fire.

"Damnation!" she cursed, hurrying over. She looked around her in panic. There was nothing she could use to grasp the hot iron skewer without burning herself.

"Nay, I'm not about to let you go to waste."

Whipping the blanket off her shoulders, she wrapped one corner of it around her hand and arm and reached for the rod. After a couple of tries, she pulled the bird to safety. But in the meantime, a loose corner of the blanket found its way into the flames and was now on fire.

"Hellfire! This is not happening. We are not burning this place down."

She dropped the bird. Rolling the blanket up and throwing it onto the packed dirt floor, Elizabeth beat it with her hands and stomped on it until the fire was out.

Using the scorched blanket, she picked up their dinner off the floor and brushed off some ash clinging to the skin.

"Much better," she murmured. "Who says cooking is an art?"

But as she turned to put the bird on the table, her heart stopped.

Alexander stood bare-chested in the doorway.

She was as naked as Eve, as beautiful as a faerie queen.

Alexander's eyes devoured every inch of her luminous skin, lingering over every luscious curve until he realized he needed to force his lungs to breathe.

"I saved it," Elizabeth said proudly, dropping the burned carcass of the bird on the table.

To his great disappointment, she shook the blanket open and draped it around her shoulders, holding it closed over her chest as she hurried across the cottage to the bed.

"It's a wee bit burned on the skin but definitely edible," she continued.

As she leaned over the bed to pick up a dress, he had a beautiful view of her perfect, heart-shaped bottom.

"That's a good-sized goose," she called over her shoulder.

It wasn't a goose, but there was no point in correcting her. She was pretending that he hadn't been standing there, watching her. But he had been, and he knew now that there was no going back. He hadn't wanted to admit it, even to himself. He'd known it from the moment that boat sank beneath them. Perhaps even earlier, when he'd dived into that flooding river. He knew he was lying even as he told her he didn't want to marry.

Elizabeth was his, and they'd be wed in six days. The way he felt now, there would be no backing out, regardless of what they'd said to each other. He wondered how much persuasion she'd need to feel the same.

She turned, clutching the dress to her chest. He continued to stare, unable to get enough of her. The parted edges of the burned blanket gave him a clear glimpse of her long legs all the way to the hip. And then there was her face, so alert and alive, and the golden hair, loose and wild, begging for him to dig his fingers into its glowing tresses.

She was looking past him at the table, and he followed her gaze.

"I don't know why I said 'goose'. That's not goose. It's duck. I know the difference."

When he looked back at her, Elizabeth was studying him, and he realized that he was nearly as naked as she was. The blasted rain had finally stopped, so he'd rinsed the worst of the mud out of their clothes and left them, with his boots, outside to dry.

Her gaze lingered on his chest before moving slowly down past his kilt to his bare feet. Her breast rose and fell. When she looked back into his face, a blush colored her cheek.

"How did you get clean?" she asked.

"I washed in the duck pond."

"I'll do that, too."

"I'll show you where it is," he said, images of washing her clean burning in his mind. He felt himself growing hard. By the devil, he'd love to run his lips over every inch of her body.

"I saw it below the barn."

"The flood waters are still rising," he told her. "They're nearly to the pond itself."

"I'll manage."

She started to move past him to the door, but before he knew what he was doing, he grabbed her by the waist and pulled her in one sweeping motion against him.

She gasped and he kissed her, a hard kiss that ended before she could even think of fighting him. He pulled back.

But she wasn't fighting him. She didn't move. Her face was inches away from his. Her eyes wide. One palm slowly flattened against his chest. He could have sworn she'd stopped breathing entirely. But her heart was beating so hard that he could hear it, or was that the sound of his own heart?

"You're so beautiful," he murmured against her lips, staring into her blue eyes. He brushed a finger across her dirt-spattered cheek and touched her lips, still wet from his kiss. He felt her shudder.

His mouth lowered to hers again, this time tenderly, caressingly.

"Elizabeth."

He dug his fingers into her hair, cupping the back of her neck, teasing the seam of her lips with his tongue.

A soft moan escaped her throat. That sound of surrender was the sweetest he'd ever heard. Her eyes closed. He deepened the kiss, thrusting into the sweet opening of her mouth, exploring. She trembled in his arms, her body becoming soft and molding to his.

He wanted to cast aside the blanket and the dress that separated them. He wanted to bury himself deep inside her.

She drew back from the kiss and looked into his eyes.

"I'll be back," she whispered.

11

RISING from the clean waters of the pond, Elizabeth squeezed the excess from her hair, dried herself, and pulled the wool dress over her head.

Above her, the evening sky was turning from an opaque blue to red gold as the sun descended in the west. The summer air was fresh and clear. If it weren't for the waters covering the fields and the rivers running down from the forests, one would have a hard time believing a tempest had just passed.

But the storm inside her continued to rage. When she thought of Alexander's kiss, Elizabeth's heart pounded. Her body ached in unmentionable places. Her lips tingled, and she could still feel the breathless sensation.

Passion. She'd never known it. Before today, she'd never allowed herself to lose control, to shut down all logic, to silence reasonable fears. She understood it now, glancing up at the open door of the cottage. She wanted him. She wanted Alexander to kiss her again. She wanted more than that.

Two of her could have fit inside the dress, but Elizabeth

wasn't surprised. The farm's mistress was expecting. She'd find something to belt it tighter. Her wet hair was in disarray, but it didn't matter. Her body was clean.

Her body.

A long breath flowed out of her. She hugged her arms around her chest, recalling the longing ache in her breasts when he kissed her, the liquid heat moving inward through her limbs, gathering at the junction of her legs. Indeed, she wanted him to do more. She wanted him to do the things a husband does to a wife.

Husband? Picking up the blanket, she started toward the cottage, enveloped now in the golden light of sunset.

At this moment, palace life and the world she'd known seemed so far away. Benmore Castle and the Highlands held a future that was not so daunting, after all. At least, not if Alexander were there with her. That was the crux of it, that man waiting up the hill in that cottage. She wanted to be with him. But what did he want?

"Halloo!"

Elizabeth's stomach sank as she whirled around. Two men waved at her from a flat-bottomed boat in the flooded field below the duck pond. They were still some distance away but she recognized the queen's colors. Castle guards.

"Hellfire," she murmured, disappointment washing through her. It was too soon. She didn't want to be found right now.

Elizabeth took a step back.

"We're searching for a lady from the castle," one man shouted up to her.

"No ladies here," she replied, putting on her best Stirlingshire accent.

"There might be a Highlander with her," the other man called out. "A bear of a man, he is. You can't mistake him."

Panic rose like bile into her throat as they drew even

closer. If they were rescued now, would all they'd been through be enough for Alexander to change his mind? She couldn't chance it. They needed more time together.

"Nay, no Highlanders. No bears either."

The boat bumped, bottoming on a shallow place offshore. As one man used an oar to free the craft, the other peered at her.

"Mistress Hay?"

Elizabeth shook her head and took two steps back. Her mind raced. If she turned and ran, they'd come after her for certain. She wasn't ready to return to the castle.

"Aren't you the queen's friend, mistress?"

"Nay. Not I, sir."

The two men were staring at her.

"You're not Mistress Hay?"

"Are you daft?" She motioned toward the cottage. "Do I need to fetch my husband?"

The queen's guards exchanged a look.

She waved them off. "You'd best be on your way if you're to get back to Stirling before nightfall."

Elizabeth waited until they turned the boat. Shaking out and refolding the blanket, she watched them move away toward the river.

Standing inside the open cottage door, Alexander banged his fist into his palm. His spirit soared as he listened to Elizabeth choose to stay with him over going back to Stirling Castle. He had his answer.

He'd watched Elizabeth from the moment she made her way down to the duck pond. He'd seen her bathe and dress. And he'd spotted the small boat crossing the flooded fields.

When the castle guards called out to her, he thought his time with her here had come to an end. But something made him hang back and wait. He was glad now that he did. Her response changed everything.

He ducked his head and went out into the farmyard. As she made her way toward him, he wanted to go down the hill and sweep her into his arms. But he waited, forcing himself to be still. The dress she was wearing had been made for a larger woman, but he'd never seen anything so enticing. Her bare feet and legs were visible as she lifted the hem above the rain-drenched ground. She smiled at him and his body responded.

Elizabeth was inexperienced. He needed to give her time, go slowly, woo her. But before the sun went down, that dress would be history and those golden tresses falling in waves to her waist would be the only thing covering her. Other than his body.

"Who were they, those men in the boat?" he asked as she drew near.

"Guards from Stirling. They wanted to know if we needed help."

"What did you tell them?"

"I sent them away," she said. "I told them the duck on our table wasn't large enough to feed four."

She looked over her shoulder at the disappearing boat, and Alexander saw the pulse beating wildly at her throat. She was avoiding his gaze.

"I'm starved," she told him. "Did you eat that entire bird while I was bathing?"

"I thought I'd wait for you."

He followed her in, knowing that despite what she'd told the castle guards, their time in the cottage was nearly over. Those men were not fooled. By morning, others would surely be arriving. In all likelihood, the cotters who lived here would return, as well.

He sat himself across the table. Elizabeth drew the

skewer from the duck and busily cut the bird into sections, pushing his supper across the table to him. As they ate in silence, he never took her eyes from her. She seemed confident, at ease with the simplicity of their setting, happy with the little that they had.

While she was sleeping, he'd busied himself taking care of the animals and preparing the duck. But before going out, he'd taken a moment to watch her sleep. Her beauty took his breath away. And then there was their kiss. He was intoxicated with her, impatient to drink more of her lips. He wanted to taste the most private parts of her.

A warm breeze wafted through the cottage, pushing a strand of blond hair across her cheek. He reached across and tucked it behind her ear, caressing the delicate line of her jaw.

She was sitting quite still, her eyes open wide.

"You've surprised me," he said, breaking the silence. "And that doesn't usually happen."

"I could say the same."

"Battling the storm and everything else, you've shown me you're a woman of strength and courage."

"And I'm handy with an oar," she said, smiling.

"Aye, that too."

He wasn't about to let her be distracted. He wanted her in that bed. He wanted her body beneath his. He could already feel his cock buried deep within her. But he needed to get all the business behind them. They were done with their dinners. He swept the bones aside with the back of his hand.

"I had another reason for coming to Stirling."

"Breaking our contract wasn't enough?" she asked, a trace of sadness flashing across her face.

"I don't need any contract to tell me what to do. I don't believe you do, either."

She didn't deny it. They had come to a place far beyond pretending.

But there were things she needed to know and, seeing the sand slip through the hourglass, Alexander charged ahead.

"The king is arriving this week. He has commanded me to come and speak with him."

Her eyebrow shot up in surprise. "Do you know why?"

"James intends to rebuild and reorganize his navy, with me as Lord Admiral."

She folded her hands together on the table. Alexander tried to imagine everything that might be running through her mind. He could almost read in her face the fears she'd spoken of when she told him she didn't want to marry him.

"What will the position entail?" she finally asked.

He knew the real question was how the king's offer would affect her.

"In taking it, I'll have less time at Benmore Castle. And less time with my wife."

Elizabeth sat pensively, her gaze drifting to the open window.

He didn't want to lose her now, allowing her to imagine the worst while he was still contemplating his options.

"But I haven't yet decided to accept the offer."

"Why wouldn't you take it?"

"I have many things to consider. For one, I'm not convinced my temperament is best suited to the task."

"But he sought you out. That's a great honor."

"Do you know the king?"

"I don't know him," she admitted. "He's never once joined Queen Margaret here since I arrived at Stirling. It's become clear to me that they don't have an amicable marriage."

"There are reasons for their estrangement," he asserted.

"The attention she gets from clans infuriates him. The Highlanders have a devotion to her that he's never known."

And that wasn't only true among the northern folk. Across the realm, the king's costly and unrealistic schemes had made him an unpopular ruler.

"I've met many nobles who have been alienated by him," she said. "Some are members of his immediate family."

"The weakness in his character and his judgment makes him surround himself with pandering sycophants. And it's a constantly changing circle."

This was at the heart of his problem, Alexander realized. Temperament be damned. How could he become Lord Admiral of the king's navy when he had so little respect for the man who put him in charge?

"Queen Margaret is very different," she said. "But I've seen his favoritism firsthand. The king's older son lives here at Stirling, ignored by his own father."

Another link in the chain of mistakes that seemed to be defining this king's reign.

"Only a wee, insecure man would be jealous of his son and his own wife. Word is if Margaret says the sky is blue, he'll say it's black just to spite her." Alexander frowned. "But court politics can be a deadly business."

He stretched out his legs under the table and they rubbed against hers. Elizabeth sat up straight, drawing her legs in. He feared what they'd gained might be lost. He had to make her understand that nothing was final as it now stood, and if there was a matter of choosing, there would be no competition. He'd marry her in a heartbeat and forfeit the king's favor.

"Queen Margaret thinks very highly of you," she said. "She's the one who devised the plan for me to take you to the abbey."

"To meet my friend, Sir Robert Johnstone." He smiled.

"I think she made certain we'd never get that far. Those children calling me 'Mum'. The queen's guards turning their backs. The scared blacksmith who couldn't get away fast enough once you came after us," she scoffed. "She has romantic ideas about knights coming to the aid of damsels in distress."

"I like the way things have turned out," he said, reaching across the table and taking her hand. "I'll have to thank her for putting you and me here together."

She met his gaze.

"Alone," he drawled.

He reached over and traced her bottom lip with his thumb. She didn't draw away from him, and he felt a tremor go through her.

"Alone in this cottage where I can ravish you . . . on that bed, on this table, here on my lap."

Elizabeth's chest rose with her sharp intake of breath. He held her gaze. He wanted to take her now, and it was only right that she know it.

"But before all of that, let's settle one thing." He kissed her palm. "Will you marry me?"

"I'm still a Lowlander."

"You and I have been promised to each other for decades. My clan considers you one of us. They want you there at Benmore Castle," he told her. "And remember, you have iron in your will and brains in your head. The Macphersons will be lucky to have you."

Her cheeks burned. Her fingers entwined with his.

"Marry me, Elizabeth."

❧ 12 ❧

AFTER SO MANY YEARS, their lives had collided. Like two raindrops falling through the air side by side, they struck the surface of this flooded pond, splashed, and then melded together into something greater.

They each had desires, responsibilities, and dreams; but now they had entered a life of new possibilities, and Elizabeth knew that they must now come together, work together, to make it all a reality.

Alexander's profession would take him far from her. There was no denying that. If she were to marry him, they would be spending time apart. If she were to accept his offer, Elizabeth would have to be strong. She would need to be confident and ready to embrace his clan. Sometimes with him, sometimes alone, she would have to build a future for them all.

Two days ago, the prospect terrified her. She had plans, a different future in mind. Most importantly, she didn't know the character of the man who was her intended. But so much had happened. And it wasn't the danger of the storms or surviving this adventure together that finalized her decision. It was meeting the man beyond the daunting reputation . . . and understanding the woman lurking within her own skin.

For twenty-three years, she'd been an observer of life. Whether she was accompanying her father on his many projects or living at Queen Margaret's court, she'd watched from a safe distance—learned some things—but never immersed herself completely. She'd never created anything of her own. Now she had a chance. As long as he was hers and she was his—for one day or for eternity—Elizabeth was ready. Those possibilities lay within their grasp.

"I'll marry you, Highlander," she told him. "But from time to time, would you take me aboard your ship if I promise to learn to swim?"

He laughed and his shoulders relaxed. The hard line of his jaw softened. She hadn't realized until this moment that he'd been anxious about her answer.

"I'll teach you to swim," he replied. "And I'll take you with me wherever I go. Whenever you like."

Still holding her hand, he got up and came around the table. She stood, her insides whirring in sweet turmoil about what she knew was to come. Never, before meeting Alexander, had she thought of the inevitability of this moment. No other man had ever made her insides tremble like this.

She stared at his lips, remembering the pressure of them on her own.

"Touch me, Elizabeth."

Desire ripped through her. An intense, primitive need started low in her belly, spreading like fire through her limbs.

She reached out, touching his chest, running her fingers over the taut sinews, over a scar as long as her hand. His muscles and skin reacted to her feathery touch. She slid her hand lower to his abdomen where dark hair formed a triangle and disappeared at the belt. She traced it downward.

She was aware of her breaths coming in shallow gasps, but then so were his.

He took hold of her hands and pulled them around his waist, drawing her closer until their bodies met. Through the layers of the dress and his kilt, she felt the pronounced ridge of his erection. Warmth licked through her limbs. She wanted to melt and mold herself against his body. She traced the hard lines of muscle on his back.

"There's only so much I can take this first time," he said.

"Will there be more than one time?" she asked coyly.

His lips descended on hers, kissing her with a passion that scorched her. In all her life, she had never known this yearning that he ignited in her. It was a fire that only made her want to burn hotter. The throb that had started in her belly became white hot, pulsing deliciously. Elizabeth wanted him to take her . . . right here, this moment.

"A second time," he growled. "And a third too, if you give me time. You can have your way with me as many times as you desire."

He scooped her up into his arms and carried her across the cottage.

With every step, his mouth brushed her neck, leaving a tingling wake along her skin and spreading a delicious ache through her body. When he stood her beside the bed, he held her tightly to him, his thigh pressing intimately between her skirts. Raw need rushed through her center. It was like running headlong down a hill, crazy and out of control. Elizabeth tried taking steadying breaths to slow and prolong the fiery madness.

He pulled the dress slowly over her head, dropping it at her feet. She saw his eyes darken. Her body reacted to the caress of his gaze, prickles of heat following the path of his eyes. Her skin, her flesh strained to be touched.

"You take away my breath with your beauty," he said.

"You've seen me naked before."

He looked hungrily into her flushed face, his thumb moving down the column of her neck. "But have I touched you before?"

"You did, brushing away the bees. Don't you remember? You . . ."

Elizabeth forgot what she was about to say when a finger traced a slow seductive line to her breasts. His palms cupped the weight of each, his thumbs circling the sensitive nipples.

"Did I taste you before?" he asked as his mouth closed over one.

She cried out softly at the tug of his lips. Her breaths shortened as she threaded her fingers into his hair. She watched in amazement the hard planes of his handsome face against the curves of her flesh.

"I think . . . I think I would have remembered this."

Alexander smiled as he gently sat her down on the bed and stepped back.

He unfastened his belt. Elizabeth watched his hands' movements. He unwrapped the kilt from his hips and dropped it to the floor.

Elizabeth had seen paintings and statues of gods and heroes. She understood the male anatomy. But he was flesh and blood. He was hard, and he was larger than any Greek or Roman. Alexander Macpherson was far more impressive. And he was hers.

He came to her, and a thrill raced through her as she lay back and opened her arms to him. She shivered as an unknown excitement took control of her. Her hands traveled along his back, taking hold of his rock-hard buttocks.

She opened her legs, knowing instinctively that relief would come only when they were joined.

"Too soon," he whispered raggedly.

He took both of her hands and pushed them down onto the bed, away from her body. His mouth traveled to her breasts, laving and teasing as her tremors of exhilaration rose even higher.

Elizabeth's skin burned as his fingers brushed lazily over her stomach, moving lower until he touched the molten center of her desire.

She stopped breathing as his lips followed, sliding downward along her body. Reaching beneath her, he raised her buttocks, lifting her to his mouth.

Elizabeth's back arched and she cried out, but Alexander held her where he wanted her, tasting her. Effortlessly, mindlessly, her hips began to move to a rhythm pulsing from somewhere deep within her, and he continued to tease her until she was riding currents of passion into the very heart of a storm. Finally, with a desperate cry, she reached for him, taking hold of his hair before the madness unhinged her.

She sucked in a breath, holding it as wave after wave of pleasure swept her up until she was a leaf swirling high in the wind. She arched her back and called out his name.

"Make me yours," she cried. "I want to feel you inside me."

He moved up and kissed her even as he entered her. Her legs tightened around him, gripping him, and he drove deeply into her. He thrust hard and deep, quickening his movements until they erupted together, their cries of ecstasy blending in the warm summer night.

This is passion, she thought as her mind slowly floated back into her body.

This is love, she realized, looking into his blue eyes.

She loved Alexander. And she'd go to the edge of the world with him.

They'd come sooner than he expected.

A groundswell of feeling rushed through Alexander as he looked at Elizabeth, asleep on the bed. This was only the beginning, the start of their life, he reminded himself.

But damn them for arriving so soon, he cursed, listening to the boats moving across the flooded fields.

Stepping out into the fresh morning air, he pulled his shirt on, adjusted his kilt, and moved down to the water's edge to meet the visitors.

The flood was starting to recede, and two boats lurched through the shallows until they could get no closer to the shore. Each craft carried castle guards, and he recognized the distinguished-looking passenger in one of them. Ambrose Hay, Elizabeth's father. He was here in person to fetch his daughter.

Waiting for the old man to wade ashore, Alexander reminded himself that the three—or was it four—times he'd made love with Elizabeth last night was only a glimpse into their future. He wasn't giving her up.

Elizabeth's father had hardly stepped onto solid ground before he began his barrage of questions.

"Is it settled now?" he asked. "When my daughter lied and sent these men packing yesterday, did that mean she's decided to go through with it? Have you two come to terms? Are you to be married?"

So Elizabeth had told her father how she felt about the marriage.

"I've proposed to her and she has accepted," Alexander

said, putting the man's mind at ease. "The wedding will go on as planned."

A breath of relief exploded from Ambrose. He laughed.

"Hail to Queen Margaret. She did it. She arranged all of it."

Alexander crossed his arms over his chest. Elizabeth had already told him the part that she'd been aware of. "What do you mean, all of it? What exactly did the queen arrange?"

"I don't know what my daughter has told you, but to be honest, the lass only knew the part about leading you to the abbey." The older man grinned. "The commotion in the village, the guards walking away from Elizabeth. Everything but the attempted kidnapping was engineered by the queen. The last part was just a terrified blacksmith, acting and not thinking."

Last night, he and Elizabeth had assumed as much.

"The queen would be an excellent military strategist if she looked out the window on occasion," Alexander said wryly. "I am fairly certain she can recognize a flooded river from the White Tower."

"True. That was a dangerous game she exposed my daughter to." Ambrose looked over his shoulder at the expanded river. A moment later, he turned around again. "When Elizabeth sent away the men who came searching for you, the queen took it as a complete triumph. She sent word to me as soon as the men returned. I had no idea Queen Margaret enjoyed wielding Cupid's arrows so much. The queen planned it all to leave you two to yourself, to give you time together, hoping you'd decide to go through with the wedding. The storm and the floods only added more adventure, to her thinking."

"I'm glad we didn't worry her any," the Highlander said, not trying to hide his sarcasm.

It was a good thing he hadn't hurt anyone in the village.

Or killed someone. Alexander wondered if the queen knew about his reluctance concerning the marriage too. Not that any of it mattered any longer. Not the intrigue, not the manipulation, not the obvious flaws in the plan. It did irk him a little when he thought of how dangerous it was for Elizabeth.

Elizabeth.

He turned and looked up at the cottage. His breath caught in his chest at the sight of her standing in the open doorway.

He didn't wait for the old man and strode up the hill to her. Her gaze followed his every step. The blush on her flawless cheeks was a hint that she recalled everything they'd done last night, all that they'd said.

She reached for him and he took her hand, pressing her palm to his lips. Ambrose Hay was making his way toward them.

"As you can see, your father has arrived. We need to go back."

"Send him away," she murmured, moving into his arms and pressing her cheek against his chest. "It's too soon."

"Five days," he told her. "We'll be wed in five days."

"What if something goes wrong?"

"You are mine and I am yours. Husband and wife. Nothing can go wrong."

❧ 13 ❧

Stirling Castle
Four Days Later

"YOU'LL NOT BE MARRYING Alexander Macpherson."

She had to be misunderstanding the king's words. That was the only possibility. It couldn't be happening. None of this could be happening.

Elizabeth glanced around at the colorful assembly. At the center of it all, King James sat in the plush, carved chair his household had conveyed from Edinburgh. He motioned to the young nobleman standing by to refill his wine goblet. A musician was strumming a lyre in the corner. The monarch looked back at her.

"You've received your instructions," he said. "You're dismissed."

When she'd been summoned to the king's receiving chamber, Elizabeth hadn't any idea of the reason. But this? This was cruel. What had she done to deserve such a command? Such a punishment?

"Are you still here?" The king glared at her.

She looked at the short man perched in his oversized chair. Something about his face worried her. It was his eyes. They were alert, constantly darting about as if expecting some potential attack to materialize at any moment. Alexander was right; the man did not inspire confidence. But that didn't mean he wasn't dangerous.

"Are you deaf, woman?"

"Nay, sire. I'm only trying to take in what you said."

"I said you'll not be marrying Macpherson. It's not difficult."

The wedding was set for tomorrow. Last night after dinner, she and Alexander had stolen a few moments alone in the gardens. They'd talked about their marriage and the trip he intended to take her on around the Orkneys. He told her a second wedding celebration would take place at Benmore Castle. All good. All joyful.

And then this morning the king had arrived.

"But begging your pardon, m'lord," Elizabeth said, deciding to speak her mind. "We have a marriage contract that was signed and sealed decades ago. Our families—"

"I'm not interested in such details."

She stared for a moment, unsure of how to respond. She wished she'd met with Alexander before coming here. Did he know about this? Had he received the same abrupt command?

"If I've done something to offend Your Majesty, I beg you to tell me," she said.

"What could you do to offend me?" he scoffed. "The decisions of the monarch are as far above you as the sun is above the earth."

She loved Alexander. She would not accept this without a fight. If King James expected her to surrender their future together without an explanation, then he was truly a fool.

"Of course, sire. But if you could condescend to give me a reason for breaking this contract."

"Reason?" he barked.

"Reason," she repeated in what she hoped was a calm voice. "More than an old promise binds us, m'lord. Alexander—"

The king shot to his feet, his face aflame.

"My word is reason enough," he rasped. "But I'll tell you this. He will be my Lord Admiral, and he will marry the woman I choose. And that will be Anne, daughter of the duke of Brittany. And if you try to challenge my wishes, I shall strip Macpherson of his position and put his head on a pike. Is that reason enough?"

The silence in the chamber was chilling. Even the musician had stopped playing.

The king sat down again, picking up his wine off the table.

"Now get out, woman. You can save your wedding dress for another day."

Striding through the gates of Stirling Castle, Alexander glared up at the White Tower and vowed he would take the blasted place down stone by stone if that was what it took to find her.

The letter he'd received from Elizabeth came in answer to the message he'd sent her before the bloody storm. She was pretending as if this past week hadn't happened. That they'd never walked down the hill toward Cambuskenneth Abbey. That they hadn't been stranded by the floods. That they hadn't made love. That they hadn't planned a life together.

Elizabeth's letter said she wouldn't marry him tomorrow.

Alexander didn't need to batter down any walls. In the gardens of the Nether Bailey, he found her standing with one of the queen's companions by a low wall looking out toward the abbey. As he approached, the look on his face was enough to send the other woman scurrying.

He held the letter out. "What do you mean by this?"

And then he saw it. The swollen eyes. The tears running down her face.

"Elizabeth, what's wrong?"

He didn't give her a chance to protest but took her into his arms. She came willingly as sobs wracked her body.

"Talk to me. Why this letter? What has upset you?"

It was some time before she could catch her breath and speak. She pulled away and looked up at the castle buildings. "Not here. Someone might see us."

"I don't care if the whole bloody court sees us," he told her. "Why should we hide?"

Elizabeth took him by the hand and drew him into an alcove by the stairs. Perplexed, he ran a thumb under her eyes and lifted her chin. It broke his heart to see her so distraught. He brushed his lips against hers and tasted the saltiness of the tears.

"Tell me," he said.

She put her forehead against his chest for a moment and then looked up at him. "The king summoned me this morning. He has commanded that I not marry you."

If Elizabeth were not so upset, he would have laughed out loud. For a wee man, James Stewart had stones the size of cannonballs. They were far more impressive than the pea-sized brain he had rattling around in his skull.

But Alexander didn't laugh. He couldn't. Everything made sense now. He understood Elizabeth's letter.

"The haughty worm said the same thing to me this morning," he told her. "He must not have been too pleased with my answer, so he came after you."

"What did you tell him?"

"I told him I had no wish to be Lord Admiral of his navy. I'd not be part of rebuilding a fleet for him. I'm not the man for him. And I'll not marry anyone but you."

Her blue eyes shone with tears. "You said that?"

"Aye, but it looks like I should have taken him by the throat instead." He wiped away the wetness from her silky cheeks. "And if the man were worth my time, I would have told him that no title or wealth would ever convince me to walk away from the greatest treasure in my life. Nay, Elizabeth. We'll marry tomorrow. He cannot spoil that."

"But he can," she cried out as fresh tears appeared. "He threatened your life if I disobey."

Alexander wasn't surprised that the king wouldn't make the same threat to him face-to-face. But the petulant coward had no compunction about frightening Elizabeth with his empty words.

"James is a scoundrel and a fraud, my love, and a petty one at that. He's only saying these things because I turned him down and because Margaret has been crowing about bringing us together."

"But he threatened your life," she repeated. "He'll put your head on a pike. He told me!"

"Let him try. He can't do it."

She shook her head. "He's the king, Alexander. He can do what he wishes."

"And I am Macpherson of Benmore Castle," he said firmly. "I am a Highlander, with more allies among the nobility of Scotland than—"

She put her fingers over his lips, hushing him. "Don't

speak treason. Don't give him any more reason to hurt you. I love you. I can't bear to have you get hurt."

"And I love you. I will drag him from the throne if I must. He won't dare step in between us."

However upset she was before, she was worse now. He frowned, realizing he'd only added to her anguish.

"I can manage this, Elizabeth. His words are empty threats."

"I can't." She shook her head, stepping away from him. "I can't do this. I love you. I can't put you in danger this way."

"Trust me, my love, when I say he has no hold on us. No power over us."

"I can't. I can't risk it."

"Tomorrow we'll be wed. And you'll see it for yourself. He's tried to create an illusion to frighten you. Something that cannot be."

"Nay," she wept. "I won't do it."

"Elizabeth!"

"I won't be there tomorrow," she cried, running off.

They say there are no secrets in a castle. Elizabeth didn't know how it was that her father learned of her torment, but she was glad when he came to her. She needed help. She needed advice on how to seal up the gaping hole in her heart.

She loved Alexander. But she could not understand his recklessness when it came to the king's threats.

As she sat side by side with Ambrose on the bench in a private corner of the castle's gardens, the entire story tumbled out. She told him everything the king said. She told him of Alexander's attitude.

"Do you understand now why I'm so miserable?" she

asked. "Do you see why I cannot go to the church for my own wedding?"

"I understand," the old man said quietly. "Why haven't you brought this to Queen Margaret's attention?"

"That would be a mistake. The queen has no influence over King James. Her involvement would only complicate the situation and make it worse."

"That is quite astute of you." Ambrose nodded. "Now you say Alexander is not responding reasonably to this threat."

"The man is a warrior. He fears nothing. He thinks he is invincible. He has no respect for the power of the king. He believes this is simply a battle of wills that he can win."

"And you don't?" her father asked. "You don't trust his judgment in this?"

She stood up, wringing her hands. How could she explain her fears?

"It's his life that's at risk. His life!" She started to pace. "Would he behave the same way if the king threatened to put my head on a pike? I think not."

Ambrose's face showed his outrage at the mere suggestion. "I think Macpherson would gut the king like a cod before that happened."

"Father!"

"Daughter, James Stewart is not foolish enough to make such a threat to so dangerous a man as your Alexander."

Elizabeth had been a part of court life long enough to know how dangerous the politics could be. She'd heard too much about lethal attacks in the shadows in retaliation for the slightest of insults, and imprisonment for the mere suspicion of treason. Tales were still told of all the noble heads the king had stuck on pikes both here and at Edinburgh.

"Don't be influenced by rumor," he ordered sharply as if reading her mind. "Trust him, Elizabeth."

She faced her father. "How can I when I'll be placing the noose around his neck?"

"Trust him when he tells you this is all petty maneuvering by the king."

She wanted to scream with frustration. This was petty maneuvering by a man who was no more mature than a wee child. A very dangerous and powerful child.

"The stories have been circulating for a fortnight that your nuptials wouldn't take place. But Margaret proved them all wrong." Ambrose Hay stood up and took her hand in his. "And very little irritates the king more than seeing his queen happy."

Today was the first time that she'd met the tyrant. Elizabeth had no difficulty believing that James would go to such extremes simply to annoy his spouse.

"If you do not show up at the Chapel of St. Michael tomorrow," her father continued, "no one will know that you were threatened. The court and the guests who have arrived will believe that the queen overstated her success. She will look foolish, and the king will win."

This was what the ruler of their country spent his time doing? Something so trivial? Sadly, Elizabeth knew it was the truth.

"This is life, daughter. You say you love Alexander. Trust and love are two of the pillars of a good marriage," the older man advised. "You said it yourself. He is a fearless warrior. He thinks he's invincible. Well, his achievements support that. The king's offer of leading his navy was based on Macpherson's abilities, his power, and his judgment. Don't you think it's time that you trusted him, as well?"

She did trust Alexander, but that wasn't enough. What if King James decided to arrest Alexander to make certain the ceremony tomorrow didn't happen? How far the man would be willing to go to see his wife fail?

She turned to her father. "I need your help."

"Anything. Tell me."

"I'll write another letter to Alexander this moment. Tell him that my decision is final and he'll be standing at that altar alone tomorrow. That we shall not marry." She took her father's hand. "Arrange for the letter to be intercepted and read by the king's men before it reaches my intended."

14

Stirling Castle
Wedding Day

"M'LADY," Alexander growled.

"Highlander," Elizabeth replied, coming to stand before him.

"Blast me," he cursed, tossing the veil back from her face. "You lied."

"But I came," she said, still unable to breathe past the knot in her chest. The only thing she could think of was what her defiance might bring him. "I sent that letter to make certain nothing happens to you before now."

"The seal was tampered with when I read it. It had been read by others."

"That's what I was counting on. And now we're here. But if anything happens to you . . . if he arrests you or . . . I'm afraid, Alexander!"

He brought each of her hands to his lips, pressing a kiss on her palms. "Fear nothing, my love."

Through a sheen of unshed tears, Elizabeth's eyes traveled over the magnificent warrior standing before her. And he was magnificent. Alexander's long black hair was tied back. A true Highlander, he was arrayed in his finest kilt and a shirt of gleaming white silk. A tartan of red and blue and green and white crossed his broad chest, and the bright sun flashed on the hilt of his long sword and on the clan arms inscribed on his golden brooch.

"Trust me," he said.

She tried to build her courage on the look of confidence on his handsome face. His blue eyes shone with love when they locked with hers.

"You and I forever." He placed her hand on his arm. "It's time."

The notes of the bagpipe gave way to a harp as the two stepped into the chapel. The assembled guests turned as one to greet them. Elizabeth's gaze moved to Queen Margaret, standing to the right of the altar and nodding her approval.

The knot in her chest grew larger as her gaze drifted to the left of the altar where the king stood with his entourage. His displeasure was obvious as he fixed his sharp eyes on them.

Her feet dragged, and a dread weariness filled her. She couldn't swallow, couldn't force enough air into her chest. The crowd in the chapel disappeared. In her mind's eye, she saw a scaffold, a bloodstained block, and a Highlander being hauled up the torturous steps. Her knees locked and she struggled to put one foot in front of the other. Elizabeth didn't realize that she had a death grip on Alexander's arm until he took her hand in his, entwining their fingers. His eyes met hers.

"Trust me," he said again.

Elizabeth made herself look only at the altar. They were almost there. Seven steps. Five steps. Four.

King James moved, drawing her attention. He was whispering something to the warrior towering behind him. The king's man signaled to two guards of equal size, who immediately moved closer to the monarch.

This was it. The end was here.

They reached the altar. The drum of her heart muffled the priest's voice as it rose and fell in the measured cadences of the mixed Latin and Gaelic.

Keeping the king and his men in the periphery of her vision, she could no longer focus on anything else. Would he wait for them to exchange their vows before seizing Alexander? Would they drag him from her arms? From the sanctuary of a church? Was she about to lose him forever? How could she live after doing this to him?

Elizabeth sensed a movement behind them, and she looked over her shoulder. A tall Highlander had separated himself from the crowd and was now standing behind Alexander.

"Who is that?" she asked in a whisper.

"Hugh Campbell," Alexander answered. He motioned to the priest to continue.

She heard the sound of another pair of boots coming up behind them. This time she recognized the man standing in support of their marriage. Sir Robert Johnstone, Clare's intended.

Alexander squeezed her hand reassuringly. At the sound of others approaching, Elizabeth once again glanced back and felt the knot loosen in her chest. More people kept joining them until at least a hundred nobles and warriors - Highlanders and Lowlanders - were standing in support behind them.

Elizabeth's gaze shifted to the king. His eyes were darting from her to Alexander to the army behind them. For a long moment, a brittle silence reigned in the chapel.

She held her breath, feeling only the gentle pressure of Alexander's hand.

Then, with a flick of his finger, James Stewart waved his guards back into the shadows. He nodded almost imperceptibly to Alexander and turned his face, staring at the altar.

As if nothing at all had transpired, the priest raised his hands in prayer and proceeded with the ceremony. From the grate of iron bands behind the altar, the sound of nuns' voices responded to the prayers.

When the moment came, Alexander and Elizabeth turned and faced each other as they exchanged their vows. Man and wife. Forever.

She looked up into her husband's face and remembered the journey that had brought them here. The dangers, the laughter, the passion, the trust.

"I love you, Highlander."

"I love you, Elizabeth."

Alexander lifted her off her feet and kissed away the tears on each cheek before capturing her mouth in that ageless symbol of promise and devotion and love.

When he put her down, Elizabeth realized that a crowd had queued up, eager to congratulate them. With her husband's arm around her, Elizabeth turned to the first one in line.

King James.

EPILOGUE

ALEXANDER MACPHERSON DECLINED James III's offer to serve as the Lord Admiral of his navy. The relationship between the Macphersons and the crown would improve greatly, however, throughout future generations.

James III failed to learn from his mistakes. A temperamental and short-sighted leader, he followed a misbegotten policy of courting an alliance with England. He promoted favored lackeys who served themselves and grew fat at the expense of the Scottish people. Matters only worsened when the increasingly unpopular king became totally estranged from his eldest son, the future James IV.

In 1488, the king faced a revolt. The nobles rose against him with the Crown Prince at their side. The young heir to the throne was angered by his father's favoritism toward his younger brother, and the rebel lords exploited the family rift. The king met the rebels in battle near Stirling. As his forces were defeated, James fled and was killed looking for shelter nearby.

His son, only a figurehead for the rebel army, would

become the next Stewart monarch and arguably one of Scotland's finest kings.

Alexander and Elizabeth's three sons were to play key roles in the decades that followed. Alec, their eldest, would fight beside James IV at Flodden Field. Their second son Ambrose would serve as a warrior diplomat and live to defy the English king Henry VIII. Ironically, or perhaps inevitably, their youngest son John would one day become Lord Admiral of the Navy.

The Macphersons had arrived.

Thank you for taking the time to read *A Midsummer Wedding*. If you enjoyed it, please consider telling your friends or posting a short review. Word of mouth is an author's best friend...and is much appreciated.

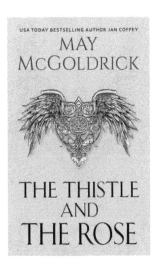

And please be sure to visit with the offspring of Elizabeth and Alexander, beginning with *The Thistle and the Rose*. In that full-length, award-winning novel, Alec Macpherson and his friend Colin Campbell become involved with a mysterious young woman who arrives with an infant at the gates of Kildalton Castle during the chaotic days following the death of the Scottish king.

AUTHOR'S NOTE

WE HOPE you enjoyed this prequel to our Macpherson Clan saga.

For the many purists and history buffs among our readers, our depiction of the marital troubles between James III and his queen, Margaret of Denmark, is fairly accurate. Of course, we hope you will accept the fiction we weave around them, and fall in love with our heroes and heroines.

After writing our first novel, *The Thistle and the Rose*, we learned from readers that they were as invested in our characters as we were. Celia Muir and Colin Campbell and Alec Macpherson lived and breathed for them.

So when we set out to write this story, we already knew so much about Alexander and Elizabeth, having introduced them to our readers as parents of their grown sons.

Also, as many of our readers know, we can never let our characters go. We hope you enjoyed this romp with our old friends in the Macpherson clan.

If you're interested in following the Macpherson Clan, here is the complete series list:

A Midsummer Wedding — the prequel to all the Macpherson series tales. Alexander Macpherson, the patriarch of the family, meets his match in Elizabeth Hay.

The Thistle and the Rose — while the smoke still lingers from the battle of Flodden Field, Colin Campbell and Celia Muir, a woman-warrior who holds the fate of Scotland in her hands, are introduced. This story is on the list of "Best Historical Romances of All Time." *Thistle* introduces Alec Macpherson, eldest son of Alexander and Elizabeth.

Angel of Skye — Alec Macpherson has served King James with his sword. Now he would give his very soul to protect Fiona Drummond from the past that haunts her and the intrigue that could change the future of Scotland.

Heart of Gold — Alec's younger brother Ambrose, second son of the Macpherson family, feels a burning desire for Elizabeth Boleyn, the exquisite natural daughter of an English diplomat. But the hated English king wants her, as well, and will stop at nothing to have her. Ambrose was introduced in *Angel of Skye*.

Beauty of the Mist — John, the youngest Macpherson brother, has been tasked with bringing home his young king's intended bride, but en route rescues mysterious Maria, adrift at sea.

The Intended — Malcolm MacLeod, Alec Macpherson's ward in *Angel of Skye,* and Jaime Macpherson, daughter of Mary Boleyn (*Heart of Gold*), have to find their way back to Scotland from the dungeons of the Tudor king.

Flame — Gavin Kerr, introduced in *Heart of Gold*, finds that the castle he has been awarded holds more than he expects, the "ghost" of the previous owner, Joanna

MacInnes, who haunts the burnt towers and the secret passages.

Tess and the Highlander (RITA© Award Finalist) — Colin Macpherson, the youngest son of Alec and Fiona (*Angel of Skye*), washes up on a remote island off the coast of Scotland, only to find a solitary young woman, Tess Lindsay.

The Highland Treasure Trilogy:

The Dreamer — When her late father was branded a traitor to the king, Catherine Percy finds sanctuary in Scotland. But a case of mistaken identity puts her in a compromising position with John Stewart, the Earl of Athol (*Flame*).

The Enchantress — Level-headed Laura Percy (the second Percy sister) takes shelter in the Highland, but when she is abducted by William Ross, the fearsome Laird of Blackfearn, all her well-made plans are torn asunder.

The Firebrand — Adrianne Percy (the youngest Percy sister) is hidden in the Western Isles, safe from her family's enemies, until her sisters send Wyntoun MacLean to return her to the Highlands. Colin Campbell and Celia Muir (*The Thistle and the Rose*) make an appearance in this exciting trilogy finale.

The Scottish Relic Trilogy:

Much Ado About Highlanders — Alexander and James Macpherson, the two older sons of Alec and Fiona (*Angel of Skye*) find more trouble than they counted on. Alexander wants his runaway bride back, but a deadly secret from Kenna Mackay's past has surfaced, and a heartless villain is closing in.

Taming the Highlander (RITA© Award Finalist) —

Innes Munro has the ability to read a person's past simply by touching them. Conall Sinclair, the Earl of Caithness, carries scars courtesy of English captors. Both of them are reluctant to let the other close, but neither can deny their growing attraction.

Tempest in the Highlands — Miranda MacDonnell is shipwrecked on the mythical Isle of the Dead with the notorious privateer Black Hawk. Alexander Macpherson and Kenna Mackay (*Much Ado About Highlanders*)play an important role, and Gillie the Fairie-Borne (*The Firebrand*) appears in the novel as he searches for his lost family.

Love and Mayhem — A hilarious medieval retelling of *Arsenic and Old Lace*, in part set in the Western Isles, with Alec and Fiona (*Angel of Skye*) making an appearance.

As authors, we love feedback. We write our stories for our readers, and we'd love to hear from you. We are constantly learning, so please help us write stories that you will cherish and recommend to your friends. Please sign up for news and updates and follow us on BookBub.

Finally, we need a favor. If you're so inclined, we'd love a review of *A Midsummer Wedding*. As you may already know, reviews can be difficult to come by these days. You, the reader, have the power now to make or break a book. If you have the time, please consider posting one to a major retailer or reading group site.

ABOUT THE AUTHOR

USA Today Bestselling Authors Nikoo and Jim McGoldrick have crafted over fifty fast-paced, conflict-filled contemporary and historical novels, along with two works of nonfiction, under the pseudonyms Jan Coffey, May McGoldrick, and Nik James.

 These popular and prolific authors write suspense, mystery, American Westerns, historical romance, and young adult novels. They are four-time Rita Award Finalists and the winners of numerous awards for their writing, including the Daphne DuMaurier Award for Excellence, the *Romantic Times Magazine* Reviewers' Choice Award, three NJRW Golden Leaf Awards, two Holt Medallions, and the Connecticut Press Club Award for Best Fiction. Their work is included in the Popular Culture Library collection of the National Museum of Scotland.

facebook.com/JanCoffeyAuthor

x.com/jancoffey

instagram.com/jancoffeyauthor

bookbub.com/authors/jan-coffey

Scottish Relic Trilogy Box Set

Love and Mayhem

18TH CENTURY NOVELS

Secret Vows

The Promise (Pennington Family)

The Rebel

Secret Vows Box Set

Scottish Dream Trilogy (Pennington Family)

Borrowed Dreams (Book 1)

Captured Dreams (Book 2)

Dreams of Destiny (Book 3)

Scottish Dream Trilogy Box Set

REGENCY AND 19TH CENTURY NOVELS

Pennington Regency-Era Series

Romancing the Scot

It Happened in the Highlands

Sweet Home Highland Christmas *(novella)*

Sleepless in Scotland

Dearest Millie *(novella)*

How to Ditch a Duke *(novella)*

A Prince in the Pantry *(novella)*

Regency Novella Collection

Royal Highlander Series

Highland Crown

Highland Jewel

Highland Sword

Ghost of the Thames

CONTEMPORARY ROMANCE & FANTASY

Jane Austen CANNOT Marry

Erase Me

Tropical Kiss

Aquarian

Thanksgiving in Connecticut

Made in Heaven

NONFICTION

Marriage of Minds: Collaborative Writing

Step Write Up: Writing Exercises for 21st Century

NOVELS BY JAN COFFEY

ROMANTIC SUSPENSE & MYSTERY

Trust Me Once

Twice Burned

Triple Threat

Fourth Victim

Five in a Row

Silent Waters

Cross Wired

The Janus Effect

The Puppet Master

Blind Eye

Road Kill

Mercy (novella)

When the Mirror Cracks

Omid's Shadow

Erase Me

NOVELS BY NIK JAMES

Caleb Marlowe Westerns

High Country Justice

Bullets and Silver

The Winter Road

Silver Trail Christmas